Shih Tzu Dogs

The Complete Owners Guide from
Puppy to Old Age

Choosing, Caring for, Grooming,
Health, Training and Understanding
Your Shih Tzu Dog

By Alex Seymour

Copyright and Trademarks

Disclaimer and Legal Notice

Foreword

Shih Tzu Dogs — The Complete Owner's Guide, from Puppy to Old Age, will answer all the questions you may have when considering sharing your home with this purebred, lovable companion breed.

As an owner, expert trainer and professional dog whisperer, I would like to teach you the human side of the equation, so you can learn how to think more like your dog and eliminate behavioral problems with your pet.

Although this breed are true lap dogs, my own Shih Tzu has stepped outside of the breed box and become the perfect working dog that truly assists us in our dog whispering business. He is an amazing testament to how incredible our relationships can be with our dogs, when they receive the proper training.

Learn everything there is to know about this breed from its royal, ancient bloodline origins to the present day companionship role this wonderful social little dog enjoys in today's modern world.

Once you've read this book you will have all the information you need in order to make a well-informed decision about whether or not the Shih Tzu is the breed for you, and you will know how to care for them every stage of their life.

Acknowledgments

In writing this book, I also sought tips, advice, photos and opinions from many experts of the Shih Tzu breed.

In particular I wish to thank the following wonderful experts for going out of their way to help and contribute:

Special thanks to Susan Kilgore of Fantasy Shih Tzu, who is a true expert and breed winner at the famous Westminster Kennel Club show. Her advice and comments were greatly appreciated and culminate in a wonderful bonus chapter in which we interview her about her experiences.

Susan Kilgore of Fantasy Shih Tzu
http://www.fantasyshihtzu.com

Asia Moore of K-9 Super Heroes Dog Whispering
http://www.k-9superheroesdogwhispering.com/

Rebecca Rayner of Fluffyangel
http://www.fluffyangelshihtzus.co.uk

Pam Crump of JiDu De ShenTi Shih Tzu
http://www.pamcrump.com

Victoria Grugan of Jardhu Shih Tzu
http://www.jardhu.org.uk

Janine Scott of Honeyshuchon Shih Tzus
http://www.honeyshuchonshihtzus.co.uk

Table of Contents

Table of Contents

Table of Contents

Table of Contents

Chapter 1 - The World of the Shih Tzu Dog

History and Origins of the Breed

According to DNA studies, the lovable Shih Tzu with the long, flowing coat is one of the 14 ancient breeds of canines (dogs) originating in Tibet around 800 BC.

Depictions of the ancient Shih Tzu appear in tapestries and documents dating as far back as AD 624.

The Shih Tzu is the closest known descendant of Senji, the prehistoric Chinese wolf.

Although the exact origin and history is open for debate and can't be known for certain, there is no doubt this dog holds a special place in the hearts of all who have met them.

Many believe that the Shih Tzu breed was developed by Tibetan monks who offered the royal temple dogs as gifts to the emperors of China.

The Shih Tzu has been known by at least seven different names throughout its long history. The original, complete name of the Shih Tzu is "Tibetan Shih Tzu Kou," meaning Tibetan Lion Dog. Their lion-like facial features were revered because it is said that Buddha rode to earth on the back of a lion.

The Shih Tzu has also been named after one of the most beautiful women of China, "Xi Shi Quan," which was based on the name Xi Shi.

Most humans terribly mispronounce the name Shih Tzu — as their current modern name is of Chinese origin, it is more correctly pronounced phonetically as "She Zoo" or "Sheed-Zoo."

The name Shih Tzu refers to either one dog or many dogs as it is both singular and plural.

The Shih Tzu was raised in Chinese imperial palaces by eunuchs for the pleasure of the nobility, and anyone found owning one of these sacred dogs outside of the palace would be put to death.

During the Ming and Manchu Dynasties, Shih Tzu were used as bed warmers and placed at the feet of the emperors and empresses to generate heat on cold nights. They were so highly prized that the dogs would be allowed to dine at the Emperor's table.

Dowager Empress Tzu Hsi (Cixi), who ruled in China from 1861 through 1908, considered the Shih Tzu to be sacred. Much of the breed standard today is a result of the high standards and careful breeding in the world-renowned kennels of Pugs, Pekingese and Shih Tzu.

Empress Cixi was personally involved in the careful supervision of the breeding kennels throughout her lifetime and attempted to keep these three imperial breeds separate.

The actual breeding was carried out by palace eunuchs who, without sanction from the Empress, secretly crossed the breeds in order to both reduce the size of these dogs as well as produce unusual and desirable markings. That gave the Shih Tzu the unique characteristics that make them different from the Tibetan Lion Dogs that have become today's Lhasa Apsos.

Because the breed was kept so secret (and the fact that acquiring these sacred palace dogs was almost impossible), this resulted in the breed actually becoming almost extinct in China after the Communist revolution of 1949.

The entire gene pool of all existing Shih Tzu is made up of only 14 dogs (7 females and 7 males).

Of these fourteen Shih Tzu, three were imported from China into Norway by Mrs. Henrick Kauffman in 1932. One of the three was the only female bred in the Imperial Palace to actually make her way to the Western World.

Of the remaining foundation dogs, three Shih Tzu were imported from China when General Brownrigg was stationed in Peking, and these became the breeding stock of the Taishan Kennel of Lady Brownrigg in England.

In England during the 1930s, Shih Tzu were named after a flower and nicknamed the "Chrysanthemum Dog" because their hair grows about the face in all directions.

The first European standard for the Shih Tzu breed was written in England in 1935 by the Shih Tzu Club.

The breed was brought to the United States after World War II, when returning soldiers brought back the dogs. The Shih Tzu was recognized in America by the American Kennel Club in 1969 in the Toy Group.

Coat Colors and Types

The most commonly seen coat color in a Shih Tzu is black and white. Other colors include various shades of gold, white, black, brown, red and blue.

Many Shih Tzu fade in color as they age but can retain their general color, such as gold, red or silver. They are one of the most diverse breeds in terms of coat colors and patterns.

The only coat color that remains the same throughout the dog's life is the black and white combination with blue-black skin, but even here there are occasional exceptions.

My first Shih Tzu was black and white, which turned silver and white as the years passed, and I currently own a 6-year-old tri red, silver, and white female who has remained very close to the same since her puppyhood.

The Shih Tzu is considered to be a "hypoallergenic" breed because their silky hair does not naturally shed, however, it is usually the dog's dander (loose skin cells) or saliva that causes allergic reactions in sensitive humans.

Puppy Coats

A Shih Tzu puppy coat will be darker when they are first born and soft to the touch, and although it may drastically change color from puppy to adult (unless they are black and white), will usually remain soft or silky (although not in the case of a British Shih Tzu).

By the time the Shih Tzu puppy is approximately ten months old, they will have grown in their adult coat; if you want them kept short, now is the time to start clipping.

Adult Coats

When the Shih Tzu is growing in their adult coat, the hair will mat much more easily and you will need to brush them every single day for approximately three weeks.

The amount of brushing required by an older dog depends on the texture of the coat — it can range anywhere from every day to once a week.

Softer coats tend to tangle more quickly, particularly if they are very thick and long, so how much time you have to devote to grooming your dog each day will depend on how short or long you decide to keep their coat.

Vital Statistics

Height and Weight

The breed generally weighs between 8.6 and 16 pounds (4 to 7.25 kilograms), and their height is between 7.9 and 11 inches (20 to 28 centimeters) when measured at the withers (top of the shoulder).

Temperature

100.5 to 102.5 degrees Fahrenheit (38.05 to 39.16 Celsius) is healthy.

Respiratory Rate

The Shih Tzu takes 10 to 20 breaths per minute at rest.

Pulse

A puppy's pulse is 120 to 160 per minute; 60 to 140 per minute is typical for an adult.

Gums

These should be pink.

Litter Size

As few as 1 or as many as 12, but on average between 4 and 6 puppies are born per litter.

Lifespan

While many may live longer, on average, the Shih Tzu lifespan will be around 16 years. Generally, females will live 1.4 years longer than males.

Living Conditions

The Shih Tzu, because of their small size, does not require an expansive living environment in order to be happy. This small breed will be perfectly fine living in an apartment or condominium complex.

However, like any dog, to be well socialized and happy, they need daily exercise outside of the home in the form of at least two or three (or more) daily walks of 30 minutes or longer, depending on their age.

In order for this intelligent and sociable little companion dog to be content and well balanced, they will want to always be close to their human guardian, which means taking your Shih Tzu everywhere with you, rather than leaving them home alone for many hours in the day.

American Kennel Club Breed Standards

The American Kennel Club and other purebred registries and conscientious breeders work tirelessly to preserve breed standards, and that is why responsible breeders would never consider mixing or tampering with a breed standard just to appeal to the marketability of a fleeting fad or "designer" trend.

The official breed standard for the Shih Tzu approved by the American Kennel Club (AKC) and the American Shih Tzu Club is based on the first written standard for Shih Tzu, prescribed by the Peking Kennel Club in 1938.

As stipulated by the AKC, the Shih Tzu is a sturdy, lively, alert "toy dog" with a long, flowing, double coat.

Befitting their ancient Tibetan heritage and noble Chinese ancestry as a highly valued, prized companion and palace pet, the Shih Tzu carries itself with head held high in a proud and distinctively arrogant carriage where they carry the head well up with the tail curved majestically over the back.

In the show ring, the Shih Tzu is considered a "head breed" dog because ten of the faults are related to the head, with the rest of the dog only containing four faults (two for the legs and two for the coat).

While what makes the Shih Tzu head different are the large, round, wide-set eyes, the short, well-defined muzzle, and the nicely domed, broad, round skull, the most outstanding feature of the Shih Tzu is their temperament.

The following is the AKC breed standard for the Shih Tzu, including size, proportion, substance, coat, and gait, and all the points upon which a Shih Tzu entering a show competition will be judged:

Size — ideally, height at the withers (top of the shoulder) is 9 to 10½ inches; but, not less than 8 inches nor more than 11 inches. Ideally, the weight of mature dogs is 9 to 16 pounds.

Proportion — length between withers and root of tail is slightly longer than height at withers. The Shih Tzu must never be so high stationed as to appear leggy, nor so low stationed as to appear dumpy or squatty.

Substance — regardless of size, the Shih Tzu is always compact, solid, and carries good weight and substance.

Skull — domed.

Head — round, broad, wide between eyes, its size in balance with the overall size of dog being neither too large nor too small. Fault: Narrow head, close-set eyes.

Expression — warm, sweet, wide-eyed, friendly and trusting. An overall well-balanced and pleasant expression supersedes the importance of individual parts. Care should be taken to look and examine well beyond the hair to determine if what is seen is the actual head and expression rather than an image created by grooming technique.

Eyes — large, round, not prominent, placed well apart, looking straight ahead. Very dark. Lighter on liver pigmented dogs and blue pigmented dogs. Fault: Small, close-set or light eyes; excessive eye white.

Ears — large, set slightly below crown of skull; heavily coated.

Muzzle — square, short, unwrinkled, with good cushioning, set no lower than bottom eye rim; never downturned. Ideally, no longer than 1 inch from tip of nose to stop, although length may vary slightly in relation to overall size of dog. Front of muzzle should be flat; lower lip and chin not protruding and definitely never receding. Fault: Snippiness, lack of definite stop.

Nose — nostrils are broad, wide and open.

Pigmentation — nose, lips, eye rims are black on all colors, except liver on liver pigmented dogs and blue on blue pigmented dogs.

Bite — undershot. Jaw is broad and wide. A missing tooth or slightly misaligned teeth should not be too severely penalized. Teeth and tongue should not show when mouth is closed.

Neck, Top Line, Body — of utmost importance is an overall well-balanced dog with no exaggerated features.

Neck — well set-on flowing smoothly into shoulders; of sufficient length to permit natural high head carriage and in balance with height and length of dog.

Top Line — should be level.

Body — short-coupled and sturdy with no waist or tuck-up. The Shih Tzu is slightly longer than tall.

Chest — broad and deep with good spring-of-rib, however, not barrel-chested. Depth of ribcage should extend to just below elbow. Distance from elbow to withers is a little greater than from elbow to ground.

Dewclaws — may be removed.

Tail — set on high, heavily plumed, carried in curve well over back. Too loose, too tight, too flat or too low set a tail is undesirable and should be penalized to extent of deviation.

Shoulders — well-angulated, well laid-back, well laid-in, fitting smoothly into body.

Legs — straight, well-boned, muscular, set well-apart and under chest, with elbows set close to body.

Feet — firm, well-padded, point straight ahead.

Coat — luxurious, double-coated, dense, long and flowing. Slight wave permissible. Hair on top of head is tied up.

Trimming — feet, bottom of coat, and anus may be done for neatness and to facilitate movement.

Color and Markings — all are permissible and to be considered equally.

Gait — moves straight and must be shown at its own natural speed, neither raced nor strung-up, to evaluate its smooth, flowing, effortless movement with good front reach and equally strong rear drive, level top line, naturally high head carriage, and tail carried in gentle curve over the back.

Temperament — as the sole purpose of the Shih Tzu is that of a companion and house pet, it is essential that its temperament be outgoing, happy, affectionate, friendly and trusting toward all.

http://www.akc.org/ - (American Kennel Club)

Photo Credit: Pam Crump of JiDu De ShenTi Shih Tzu

United Kingdom Kennel Club

Note that standards all over the world can differ from the American Kennel Club Breed Standard. For example, in the United Kingdom, the UK Kennel Club Breed Standard does differ quite a lot, even in size — 8 inches to 10 inches in height — and also they stipulate small heads, long necks, narrow bodies, and long legs.

The coat is very different, being a double coat with a strong top coat like human hair but not long and silky.

The UK Kennel Club does not register tri color. The most popular color at the moment both in the show ring and with pet owners is gold and white (it used to be black and white).

http://www.thekennelclub.org.uk/ - (UK Kennel Club)

Imperial Shih Tzu

You may come across the terms Imperial Shih Tzu or Royal Imperial Shih Tzu. These Shih Tzu are bred from lines that can produce smaller, miniature puppies.

Note that the American Kennel Club, or any purebred kennel club to my knowledge, does not recognize an imperial size or teacup size Shih Tzu in its official breed standards for the dog. These smaller, undersized dogs normally are not selected or adequately screened for genetic soundness and can have many inherited issues.

Cons of Shih Tzu Ownership

The Shih Tzu is a long-lived small dog, which means that choosing to be a guardian for this toy breed also means being prepared for a long term responsibility that could be on the order of a 16- to 18-year (or longer) commitment. The small size also makes them susceptible to accidentally being injured if dropped from a height, or if pounced on by larger dogs, or even carried off by a large bird of prey.

The Shih Tzu is a non-shedding breed, which means that if you are not able to groom your dog yourself, you will need to commit to regular trips to a professional groomer every six to eight weeks.

The Shih Tzu's soft coat ideally needs to be brushed or combed on a daily basis in order to avoid tangles and matting, especially if the coat is allowed to grow long. Less daily coat maintenance will be required if the coat is kept clipped short.

The Shih Tzu is prone to teeth problems, and their teeth should be brushed every day.

A young Shih Tzu can be spirited and energetic, requiring lots of activity to keep them happy.

When not properly trained, a Shih Tzu can have a demanding personality.

Some Shih Tzu can become easily over-excited when greeting new people and dealing with new situations, which can cause them to have a reverse sneezing episode.

Pros of Shih Tzu Ownership

As a non-shedding dog, this breed is a better choice for allergy sufferers.

The Shih Tzu is relatively long-lived, which means that your pet will be your faithful companion for many years.

The small size of the Shih Tzu makes them easy to transport and more suitable for those living in an apartment without access to a yard.

The Shih Tzu is small enough to fit inside an airline-approved, in-cabin travel bag, so that they can fly with you inside the cabin.

They are a playful and cuddly, yet energetic companion who enjoys walks as well as snuggling on the couch.

The smaller size of the Shih Tzu means that they will have a smaller appetite, and therefore, a smaller budget will be required for treats and food.

The Shih Tzu is very lovable and dedicated to their family, and with their keen sense of hearing, they will always alert you to anyone approaching.

They are intelligent, eager to learn, and can be easily trained by a calm, caring guardian.

The Shih Tzu can be a good choice for a family with older children looking for a playful, yet sturdy small dog.

Why Did I Choose a Shih Tzu?

While the reasons why you might decide to choose a Shih Tzu may be quite different from why I chose this breed, you may find it interesting to know my reasons.

First, there were several practical reasons why I chose the Shih Tzu breed, including the fact that I currently live in a condominium complex that has strict rules pertaining to the size of dog permitted and requires owners to carry their dogs in common inside areas.

As well, I wanted a small dog that could easily travel with me and would fit inside a Sherpa bag, so that they would be able to ride inside the airplane cabin with me.

Further, it was important to me to have a non-shedding breed because I simply don't have a great deal of time to be vacuuming every day to pick up dog fur.

I also wanted a dog that was easy to train, but that was not classed as a "working" breed that would require excessive amounts of exercise, but had a calm and friendly nature that would be happy to work with me, without being threatening to either humans or other dogs in my capacity as a professional dog whisperer.

Finally, I chose the Shih Tzu because they are well known to be cute, cuddly, affectionate and well-mannered with both unknown dogs and humans alike, and because they live a long life.

Chapter 2 - Buying a Shih Tzu

Although a reputable breeder cannot guarantee the lifelong health of any puppy, they should be able to offer you plenty of useful information about the health of the puppy's parents.

For instance, a reputable breeder will have had their breeding dogs tested for hip, thyroid and eye problems, and prospective puppy purchasers should always inquire about possible congenital problems the parents or grandparents of the puppy might have, including any premature deaths.

Meet the Parents

Meeting the breeding parents of your new Shih Tzu puppy can tell you a great deal about what the temperament and

demeanor of your puppy will likely be when they grow into adulthood.

A Shih Tzu puppy's personality or temperament will be a combination of what they experience in the early days of their environment when they are in the breeder's care, and the genes inherited from both parents.

Visiting the breeder several times, observing the parents, interacting with the puppies and asking plenty of questions will help you to get a true feeling for the sincerity of the breeder.

Important Breeder Questions

The following is a list of the first 5 questions you should ask a prospective breeder before you decide to proceed further:

• How long have you been breeding?
• Are you certified by local Shih Tzu clubs?
• Why did you decide to breed Shih Tzu?
• Are your puppies registered?
• May I come to meet you and see your facility?

First Visit to the Breeder

If you have then made an appointment to meet with the breeder at his or her facility, the following questions will help you to get a feeling for the integrity of the breeder and whether you wish to work with them:

• Do you own both parents of your Shih Tzu puppies?

- How often do you breed the parents?
- May I meet the parents?
- Do you show your dogs?
- When will your next litter be born?
- May I see dogs you have bred?

Ask if the breeder will allow you to see the other dogs in the kennel and take note whether the kennel is clean, well maintained, and animal friendly.

Pay attention to whether the breeder limits the amount of time that you are permitted to handle the Shih Tzu puppies — a reputable breeder will be concerned for the safety and health of all their puppies and will only permit serious buyers to handle the puppies.

Check to find out if the breeder is recognized by your local, state or national breed organization.

Every reputable breeder will certainly ensure that their Shih Tzu puppies have received vaccinations and de-worming appropriate for the age of the puppies.

If you discover that the breeder has not carried out any of these procedures, or they are unable to tell you when the last shots or de-worming was carried out, look elsewhere.

Temperament Questions

You will want to choose a puppy with a friendly, easy going temperament, and your breeder should be able to help you with your selection.

Also ask the breeder about the temperament and personalities of the puppy's parents and if they have socialized the puppies.

Always be certain to ask if a Shih Tzu puppy you are interested in has displayed any signs of aggression or fear, because if this is happening at such an early age, you may experience behavioral troubles as the puppy becomes older.

Guarantee Questions

A reputable Shih Tzu breeder will be interested in the lifelong health and wellbeing of all of their puppies, and you will want to ask if you can call the breeder should a problem arise at any time during the life of your puppy.

Reputable breeders will offer return contracts to protect their reputation and also to make sure that a puppy they have sold that might display a genetic defect will not have the opportunity to breed and continue to spread the defect, which could weaken the entire breed.

If the Shih Tzu breeder you are considering does not offer this type of return policy, find one who does, because no ethical breeder would ever permit one of their puppies to end up in a shelter.

A reputable Shih Tzu breeder has nothing to hide and will be happy to provide you with references from some of his or her previous clients.

Make sure that you actually contact those people to ask them about their experience with the breeder, and inquire about the health and temperament of their Shih Tzu dog.

Also, be prepared to answer questions the breeder may have for you, because a reputable breeder will want to satisfy themselves that you are going to be a good caretaker for their puppy.

Pregnancy for Profit

The inhumane and cruel world of canine pregnancy for profit (known as puppy mills) is especially prevalent with smaller breeds such as the Shih Tzu.

Education and being very careful if buying a puppy from a pet store (I recommend against this) is the key to ensuring that you do not unknowingly become part of promoting this disreputable practice.

All the work of honest and careful breeders who strive to produce healthy puppies can quickly be destroyed by puppy mill operations that seriously contribute to overpopulation, diseases and genetically flawed puppies.

Such puppies may suffer greatly with behavioral and/or health-related problems that will cost their guardians greatly in terms of grief, stress and unexpected financial burdens. These problems may also shorten the puppy's life.

Although puppy mill puppies are sold in a variety of different locations, pet stores are the main venue. Puppies are taken away from their mothers far too young (at 4 to 5 weeks of age) and sold to brokers, who pack them into crates to ship them off, many dying during transportation.

Of course, puppy mill puppies are also sold at flea markets, through newspaper ads, and even through fancy websites and Internet classifieds.

Always be wary if you answer an advertisement and the person selling offers to deliver the puppy to you.

Important Questions

Choosing the right puppy for your family and your lifestyle is more important than you might imagine. Many people do not give serious enough thought to sharing their home with a new puppy before they actually bring one home.

For instance, many of us choose a puppy solely based on what it looks like, or because the breed may currently be popular, or because their family had the same kind of dog when they were a child growing up.

In order to be fair to ourselves, our family, and the puppy we choose to share our lives with, we humans need to take a serious look at our life, both as it is today and what we envision it being in the next sixteen or eighteen years, and then ask ourselves a few important, personal questions, which we can honestly answer, before making the commitment to a puppy. Take the time to choose wisely.

Humans who choose a dog that is not compatible with their energy and lifestyle will inevitably end up with a cascade of troubles, starting with an unhappy dog, which leads to behavioral issues, which will then lead to an unhappy family and an unhappy neighborhood.

Photo Credit: Susan Kilgore of Fantasy Shih Tzu

Pick of the Litter

Once you get to know your breeder, they will be able to help you select the right puppy for you and your family.

Beyond your gut feelings and how you may feel attracted to one puppy over all the rest, considering other factors will help improve the odds of you experiencing a positive guardianship experience with your new Shih Tzu puppy.

Some humans immediately turn into mush when they come face to face with cute little puppies, and still others become very emotional when choosing a puppy, which can lead to being attracted to those who display extremes in behavior.

Take a deep breath, calm yourself and get back in touch with your common sense, because choosing a puppy that may be very shy or frightened in the hope that if you "save" them that they may grow into a happy, well-behaved dog is not the best course of action.

Check Puppy Social Skills

When choosing a puppy out of a litter, look for one that is friendly and outgoing, rather than one who is overly aggressive or fearful.

Puppies who demonstrate good social skills with their litter mates are much more likely to develop into easy going, happy adult dogs who play well with others.

Observe all the puppies together and take notice:

Which puppies are comfortable both on top and on the bottom when play fighting and wrestling with their litter mates, and which puppies seem to only like being on top?

Which puppies try to keep the toys away from the other puppies, and which puppies share?

Which puppies seem to like the company of their litter mates, and which ones seem to be loners?

Puppies that ease up or stop rough play when another puppy yelps or cries are more likely to respond appropriately when they play too roughly as adults.

Is the puppy sociable with humans? If they will not come to you, or display fear toward strangers, this could develop into a problem later in their life.

Is the puppy relaxed about being handled? If they are not, they may become difficult with adults and children during daily interactions or during grooming or visits to the veterinarian's office.

Check Puppy's Health

Ask to see veterinarian reports to satisfy yourself that the puppy is as healthy as possible, and then once you make your decision to share your life with a particular puppy, make an appointment with your own veterinarian for a complete examination.

Before making your final pick of the litter, check for general signs of good health, including the following:

1. Breathing: will be quiet, without coughing or sneezing, and there will be no crusting or discharge around their nostrils.
2. Body: will look round and well fed, with an obvious layer of fat over their rib cage.
3. Coat: will be soft with no dandruff or bald spots.
4. Energy: a well-rested puppy should be alert and energetic.

5. Hearing: a puppy should react if you clap your hands behind their head.
6. Genitals: no discharge visible in or around their genital or anal region.
7. Mobility: they will walk and run normally without wobbling, limping, or seeming to be stiff or sore.
8. Vision: bright, clear eyes with no crust or discharge.

Hernias

Umbilical hernias are fairly common in the Shih Tzu. This is apparent as a bulge in the middle of the dog's stomach and is typically caused by the cutting of the umbilical cord too close to the abdominal wall at birth. Most will get smaller as your puppy grows up, but in some rare cases surgery is required, and this is best done at the same time as neutering/spaying.

Also check the groin area in case of an inguinal hernia — you will notice a bulge caused by tissue or abdominal organs protruding through the inguinal ring. While this shouldn't stop you buying the particular Shih Tzu, as in most cases they will be perfectly healthy, it is suggested that you do not breed further.

Best Age to Purchase a Puppy

A Shih Tzu puppy should never be removed from their mother any earlier than 8 weeks of age (at the very earliest), and leaving them until they are 10 to 16 weeks of age is preferred because this will give them the extra time they need to learn important life skills from the mother dog, including eating solid food and grooming themselves.

Also, a puppy left amongst their litter mates for a longer period of time will learn better socialization skills.

For the first month of a puppy's life they will be on a mother's milk-only diet. Once the puppy's teeth begin to appear, they will start to be weaned from mother's milk, and by the age of 8 weeks should be completely weaned and eating just puppy food.

Where to Purchase a Puppy in the USA

There are several clubs and registries that will be good starting points for learning where to purchase a Shih Tzu puppy in the United States:

The American Shih Tzu Club (ASTC) is the perfect place to start your search for a reputable breeder because they have great information about the breed, are dedicated to the future of the Shih Tzu, and have a Breeder Referral volunteer group to help prospective new owners find reputable breeders.

The ASTC also maintains a Rescue Committee with representatives in many states to help those wanting to rescue a Shih Tzu.

http://americanshihtzuclub.org/

Where to Purchase a Puppy in the UK

Kennel Club Assured Breeders (KCAB) maintains a current listing of UK registered breeders, where you can locate at least 46 Assured Breeders for the Shih Tzu.

http://www.thekennelclub.org.uk/

Average Prices for Puppies

There is a wide range of "average" pricing for any purebred dog, including the Shih Tzu, with some adoptions or rescues beginning around $300 (£180) and breeder pricing ranging between $418 and $921 (£250 and £550), or even more, depending on the particular breeder and the fees they incur for better care.

Rescue Organizations and Shelters

When you are considering rescuing a specific breed of dog or puppy, the first place to start your search will be with your local shelter and rescue groups, as well as with local Shih Tzu breeders.

You can expect to pay an adoption fee to cover the cost of spaying or neutering, which will be only a small percentage of what you would pay a breeder, and will help to support the shelter or rescue facility by defraying their costs.

Online Resources

Websites such as Petango, Adopt a Pet, and Pet Finder can be good places to begin your search.

Adopt a Pet — http://www.adoptapet.com
Petango — http://www.petango.com
Pet Finder — http://www.petfinder.com

Each of the online resources below are a central gathering site for many hundreds of local shelters, humane societies, and rescue groups.

http://www.southernshihtzurescue.org.uk
http://www.homecounties-shihtzurescue.co.uk
http://www.canadianshihtzuclub.ca/
http://www.usshihtzurescue.com/
http://www.shihtzurescue.us/

Canine Clubs

Another place to search will be Shih Tzu clubs and organizations in your local area because these groups may often have rescue dogs available.

Male or Female?

Deciding whether or not to share your life with a male or a female Shih Tzu will be an entirely personal choice that you will need to decide for your particular situation. However, there may be a few considerations that can help you to make a more informed decision.

Male dogs tend to want to mark or pee on anything upright (trees, telephone poles, tall grass, a stranger's leg) whenever they are out walking, and while a dominant female will also pee on three legs and mark territory, a male Shih Tzu, even a housebroken one, may try to lift their leg on your friend's furniture when visiting a home where other dogs are present.

While the spaying and neutering process is more invasive for females than it is for males, this is not such a tiny breed that you need to worry either way. Therefore, the best way to choose the right puppy for you will be to take your time observing the litter when you visit the breeder.

In addition, whether or not you choose to buy a puppy or a dog that is already full grown will entirely depend upon your particular circumstances, such as whether or not you want the fun of watching a puppy grow up and training them, or whether you prefer to rescue a full grown dog that should already be fully trained and socialized.

Showing a Shih Tzu

While most Shih Tzu owners have no desire to show their dogs, because it is a very big time commitment, if this is something you might enjoy, first let your breeder know your intentions so that he or she can help you to pick the right puppy from the litter.

A reputable breeder will know what characteristics to look for in a puppy that could be a good show dog, and if you are really serious about showing, you should choose a breeder who also shows dogs.

Obviously, keeping a Shih Tzu in show coat will require a great deal of dedicated work on your part, so be certain you are up to the challenge, because grooming can include weekly bathing and oiling of the coat to make the hair shine, and at the very least, you will need to provide daily brushing and combing sessions to keep debris and mats out of the longer hair.

The best way to decide whether or not you might enjoy showing your Shih Tzu will be to talk to someone who has already done so — someone who will be able to give you an accurate overview of all the ins and outs of what can be a complicated process.

Chapter 3 - Bringing Your Puppy Home

The Essential Shih Tzu Shopping List

Before bringing home your new Shih Tzu puppy for the first time, there will be a long list of items you will need to have available, including:

1. Food — the puppy will remain on whatever food they have been fed at the breeder's for at least the first couple of weeks, until they are well settled in their new home, so make sure you ask the breeder what brand to buy.
2. Food and Water Bowls — make sure they are small enough for a young Shih Tzu puppy to easily get into so that they can eat and drink without problems.
3. Kennel — when you buy your puppy's hard-sided kennel, make sure that you buy the size they will need when they are full grown. A full grown Shih Tzu will need to be able to easily stand up and turn around inside the kennel.
4. Martingale Collar, 2 Leashes and Harness — buy the harness and collar small enough to fit your puppy and buy new ones as they grow larger. You will be able to keep the same leashes as all you will ever need is a four-foot (1.22 meters) leash made out of nylon webbing, with a lightweight clip at the end (do not buy a leash that has a heavy clip on the end as it will be difficult for your small puppy to carry.
5. Soft Beds (one or two) — for them to sleep in when they are not in their kennel and large enough for a

full-grown Shih Tzu, or buy them small, and get them larger ones as they grow.

6. "Sherpa" or other type of soft-sided travel bag — to get them used to traveling inside a carrier bag, which must be large enough to fit them when they are full grown. Take it with you when you pick up your puppy from the breeder.

7. Shampoo and Conditioner — the proper pH for dogs.

8. Finger Toothbrush — this is a soft rubber cap that fits over your finger to get the puppy used to having your fingers in their mouth and their teeth regularly brushed. When they have their adult teeth, you will graduate them to a small-headed, soft toothbrush or an electric toothbrush.

9. Soft Bristle Brush and Comb — for daily grooming.

10. Puppy Nail Scissors — for trimming their toenails.

11. Small, Blunt-nosed Grooming Scissors — for trimming the hair around their eyes.

12. One or Two Soft Toys — or wait until they come home and let them pick their own toys from the pet store.

13. Puppy-sized Treats.

14. Poop Bags.

15. Pee Pads.

16. Bath Towels.

17. Non-slip Mat for the Sink or Tub.

Puppy Proofing Your Home

Unless you have chosen an extremely laid back puppy who wants to sleep more than explore, most puppies will be a curious bundle of energy, which means that they will get into everything within their reach.

As a responsible puppy guardian, you will want to provide a safe environment for them, which means eliminating all sources of danger, similar to what you would do for a curious toddler.

Power cords to a teething puppy may look like irresistible, fun, chew toys. Keep all power cords out of your puppy's reach or enclose them inside a chew-proof PVC tube.

Kitchen: there are many human foods that can be harmful to puppies and dogs. Teach them boundaries by calmly sending them out of the kitchen any time you are preparing food, and they will quickly get the idea that this area is off limits to them.

Bathroom: low bathroom cupboards and drawers or the side of a bathtub where you may leave your shaving supplies can hold many dangers or accidents waiting to happen for a young and curious Shih Tzu puppy.

Kleenex, cotton swabs, toilet paper, razors, pills and soap left within your puppy's reach are an easy target that could end up in an emergency drive to your veterinarian's office.

Jewelry, hair ties, bills, coins, medications and other items small enough for a puppy to swallow are also dangerous items to leave lying about where a puppy can reach them.

Living Room: books and magazines, pens, pencils, crayons, coasters, iPods, TV remotes, slippers and more have a strange way of making their way inside a puppy's mouth.

Plants: can be a very tempting target for your puppy's teeth, so you will want to keep them well out their reach. Move floor plants to a shelf or counter, or place them behind a closed door.

Garage and Yard: there are obvious as well as subtle dangers that could seriously harm or even kill a Shih Tzu puppy that are often found in the garage or yard.

Some of these include antifreeze, gasoline, rat, mice, snail and slug poisons, weed killers, paint, solvents, grass seed, bark mulch, fertilizers, pesticides and insecticides.

Bottom line, anything that can fit inside your puppy's mouth needs to be kept out of their reach, which means keeping your home free of excess clutter, so that the only temptations your puppy sees are those which they are allowed to have.

Puppy's First Night

Before you go to the breeder's to pick up your new Shih Tzu puppy, vacuum your floors (even under the beds) and do a last minute check of every room to make sure that everything that could be a puppy hazard is out of sight.

Close off most of the rooms inside your home, leaving just one or two rooms that the puppy will have access to.

Get out your supply of puppy pee pads and have them at the ready for when you bring your little companion home. Leave a soft puppy bed in an area where you will be spending most of your time and where your puppy will easily find it. If you have already purchased a soft toy, take the toy with you when you go to pick up your puppy.

TIP: take either your hard-sided kennel or your soft-sided travel bag with you when going to bring your new Shih Tzu puppy home, and make sure that it is securely fastened to the seat of your vehicle with the seatbelt restraint system.

Resist the urge to hold your new Shih Tzu puppy in your lap on the drive home. Instead, ask a friend to go with you, so they can drive you and the new puppy home. This way you can sit close to them on the back seat.

Place them inside their kennel or bag with their new toy, which will be lined with soft towels and perhaps even a warm, towel-wrapped hot water bottle (and a pee pad on top), and close the door. If they cry on the way home, remind them that they are not alone with your soft, soothing voice.

TIP: before bringing your new Shih Tzu puppy inside your home, first take them to the place where you want them to relieve themselves and wait it out long enough for them to at least go pee.

Then bring them inside and introduce them to the area where their food and water bowls will be kept (NOT inside the kitchen), in case they are hungry or thirsty.

Let them wander around sniffing and checking out their new surroundings and gently encourage them to follow you wherever you go.

Show them where the puppy pee pad is located and place it near the door where you will exit to take them outside to relieve themselves. Many pee pads are scented to encourage a puppy to pee, and if they do, happily praise them.

Show them where their hard-sided kennel is (in your bedroom) and put them inside with their soft toy, with the door open, while you sit on the floor in front and quietly encourage them to relax inside their kennel.

Practice this kennel exercise several times throughout the day, and if they will take a little treat each time you encourage them to go inside their kennel, this will help to further encourage them to want to go inside.

After they have had their evening meal, take them outside approximately 20 minutes later to relieve themselves, and when they do, make sure you are very enthusiastic with your praise and perhaps even give a little treat.

So far your Shih Tzu puppy has only been allowed in several rooms of your home, as you have kept the other doors closed, so keep it this way for the first few days.

Before it's time for bed, again take your puppy outside for a very short walk to the same place where they last relieved themselves, so that they can smell what they are supposed to do there, and make sure that they go pee before bringing them back inside.

Before bed, prepare your Shih Tzu puppy's hot water bottle and wrap it in a towel so that it will not be too hot for them, and place it inside their hard-sided kennel.

Play soothing music in the background and turn the lights down low while you invite your puppy to go inside their kennel with their soft toy. Let them walk into the kennel under their own power, and when they do, give them a little treat (if they are interested) and encourage them to snuggle down to sleep while you are sitting in front of the kennel.

Once they have settled down inside their kennel, close the door, go to your bed and turn all the lights off. It may help your puppy to sleep during their first few nights home if you continue to play quiet, soothing music.

If they start to cry or whine, stay calm and have compassion, because this is the first time in their young life without the comfort of their mother or their litter mates.

This is a very dangerous times for humans, who will usually give in and take the puppy to bed with them. Be strong, and do not let them out of their kennel. Simply reassure them with your calm voice that they are not alone until they fall asleep.

With regard to the Shih Tzu sleeping inside their kennel in your bedroom — this is the best place for them as all dogs are pack animals and to lock them outside of your bedroom at night can be traumatizing for them, because to be happy, they need to follow their leader (i.e. the dog guardian). This is not a noisy, smelly or large dog, and they will be just fine in their small kennel in your bedroom.

The other alternative, once they are house trained, would be to allow them to choose their own sleeping spot (so long as it's not on your bed), such as your couch.

Puppy's First Week

During the first week, you and your new Shih Tzu puppy will be getting to know one another's habits and settling into your new routine together.

Make this new transition time as easy as possible on you both by maintaining a consistent waking and sleeping routine, so that both of you will easily get into the rhythm of your new life together.

As soon as you wake in the morning, hurry into your outdoor clothes, remove your puppy from their kennel and take them immediately outside to relieve themselves at the place where they went pee before bed last night.

If you are teaching them to ring a doorbell to alert you that they need to go outside, let them ring the bell before you go out the door with them, whether you are carrying them, or whether they are walking out the door on their own.

TIP: during the first week, you may want to carry your puppy outside first thing in the morning, as they may not be able to hold it for very long after waking up.

When you bring them back inside, you can let them follow you on the leash so they get used to their new collar, leash and/or harness arrangement.

Be very careful not to drag your puppy if they stop or pull back on the leash. If they refuse to walk on the leash, gently hold the tension toward you (without pulling) while encouraging them to walk toward you until they start to move forward again.

Now it will be time for their first feed of the day, and after they have finished eating, keep a watchful eye on the clock, because you will want to take your puppy outside to relieve themselves in approximately 20 minutes or less.

When your Shih Tzu puppy is not eating or napping, they will want to explore and have little play sessions with you, which will be important opportunities that will help you bond with your puppy a little more each day.

As their new guardian, it will be your responsibility to keep a close eye on your puppy throughout the day, so that you get to know their body language and will notice when they need to relieve themselves, so that you can direct them to their pee pad or take them outside.

Pay close attention and make sure that they are eating and drinking enough throughout the day. An easy way to do this is to set regular feeding times at least three times a day, which works out quite nicely for us humans who usually like to eat breakfast, lunch, and dinner.

Set specific times when you will take your puppy out for a little walk on leash and harness, so that they are not only going outside when they need to relieve themselves, but so that you are giving them the opportunity to learn about the outside world in a disciplined manner, by following you while they explore their new neighborhood.

Do not expect a very young Shih Tzu puppy to walk with you for a long time, as they will get tired easily, so keep your walks to no more than 15 or 20 minutes during your first weeks and if they seem tired or cold, pick them up and carry them home.

TIP: a young Shih Tzu puppy will get cold very quickly if they become wet.

Common Mistakes to Avoid

Sleeping in Your Bed

Many of us humans crumble like a cheap deck of cards when we hear a crying puppy and make the mistake of allowing them to sleep with us in our bed. While this may help to calm and comfort a new puppy, it will set a dangerous precedent that can result in behavioral problems later in life. As well, a tiny Shih Tzu puppy can easily be crushed by a sleeping human body.

A little tough love at the beginning will help them to learn to both love and respect you as their leader.

Realize that you may not get very much sleep those first few nights and may end up sleeping on the floor beside the kennel to calm your lonely puppy.

TIP: if your bed is big enough and there is no danger of the kennel falling onto the floor in the middle of the night, you might try placing your puppy's kennel beside you on your bed until they get used to their new kennel routine.

Picking Them Up at the Wrong Time

Never pick your puppy up if they are showing fear or aggression toward an object, other dog or person, because this will be rewarding them for unbalanced behavior.

Instead, remember that your puppy is learning from watching you and "reading" your energy, therefore, how you react in every situation, and your energy level, will affect how your puppy will react.

In other words, if they are doing something you do not want them to continue, your puppy needs to be gently corrected by you, with firm and calm energy so that they learn not to react with fear or aggression.

Playing Too Hard or Too Long

Many humans play too hard or allow their children to play too roughly or too long with a young puppy.

It's very important to remember that a young puppy tires very easily and especially during the critical growing phases of their young life. They need plenty of rest while they grow into their adult bodies.

With regard to toys for them, I don't think there is any "best" toy. My Shih Tzu still plays almost exclusively with the soft toy he picked out himself when he was just 10 weeks old, even though he is now 8, and even though he has other toys he could choose. It is personal choice.

Hand Games

Too many humans get into the habit of playing the "hand" game, where you rough up the puppy and slide them across the floor with your hands, because it's amusing for humans to see a little ball of fur scrambling to collect themselves and run back across the floor for another go.

This sort of "game" will teach your puppy to disrespect you as their leader in two different ways — first, because this "game" teaches them that humans are their play toys, and secondly, this type of "game" teaches them that humans are a source of excitement.

When your Shih Tzu puppy is teething, they will naturally want to chew on everything within reach, and this will include you.

As cute as you might think it is when they are young puppies, this is not an acceptable behavior and you need to gently, but firmly, discourage the habit, just like a mother dog does to her puppies when they need to be weaned.

Have compassion for your puppy during teething time, as their gums are sore and they need to chew to help relieve the pain — just make sure the pain is not being transferred to you as those milk teeth are razor sharp.

A light flick with a finger on the end of a puppy nose, combined with a firm "NO" when they are trying to bite human fingers, or any other parts of human anatomy, will discourage them from this activity. Then immediately give them something they CAN chew such as a chew toy.

If the puppy persists in chewing on you, remove yourself from the equation by getting up and walking away. If they are really feisty and persistent, put them inside their kennel with a favorite chew toy until they calm down, or take them out for a walk to burn off some of that energy.

Always praise your puppy when they stop inappropriate behavior, as this is the beginning of teaching them to understand rules and boundaries.

Often we humans are quick to discipline a puppy or dog for inappropriate behavior, but we forget to praise them for their good behavior.

Free Feeding

While free feeding a young puppy can be a good idea until they are about four or five months old, what is NOT a good idea is allowing an adult dog to continue to eat food any time they want by leaving food out for them 24/7. Remember, this is a dog, not a cat.

Free feeding can be a serious mistake, as every dog, including a Shih Tzu, needs to know that their guardian is absolutely in control of their food.

If your Shih Tzu does not associate the food they eat with you, they may become picky eaters or think that they are the boss, which can lead to other behavioral issues later on.

Treating Them Like Fur Children

Another particularly bad habit small dog owners get into is treating their Shih Tzu like small fur humans.

When humans do not honor their canine companions for the amazing dogs they are, and try to turn them into small fur people, this can cause them much stress and confusion that could lead to behavioral problems.

Remember that the one thing that a Shih Tzu (or any dog) is the very best at being is a dog.

A well-behaved Shih Tzu thrives on rules and boundaries, and when they understand that there is no question you are their leader and they are your follower, they will live a contented, happy and stress-free life.

Bonding With Your Shih Tzu

Do not make the mistake of thinking that "bonding" with your new Shih Tzu puppy or dog can only happen if you are playing or cuddling together, because the very best bonding happens when you are kindly teaching rules and boundaries, or showing them a new trick.

You will begin bonding with your Shih Tzu puppy from the very first moment you bring them home from the breeder, because you will be teaching them that safe vehicle travel means being inside their Sherpa or kennel.

This is the time when your puppy will be the most distraught, as they will no longer have the guidance, warmth, and comfort of their mother or their other litter mates, and you will need to take on the role of being your new Shih Tzu puppy's center of attention.

Be patient and kind with them as they are learning, because they have just been removed from all they have known and entered a totally strange, new world where they will now learn that you are their entire universe, and they must learn to safely navigate foreign surroundings.

Your daily interaction with your puppy during play sessions and especially your disciplined exercises, including going for walks on leash, and teaching commands and tricks, will all be wonderful bonding opportunities that will bring you even closer together.

Chapter 4 - Potty Training

Human Training

Whether you call it house training, house breaking, or potty training, there are many different methods for helping your Shih Tzu puppy to quickly learn that their bathroom is outside rather than inside your home.

The following are methods that you may or may not have considered, all of which have their own merits, including:

• Bell training
• Exercise pen training
• Free training
• Kennel training

All of these are effective methods, so long as you add in the one critical, and often missing "wild card" ingredient, which is "human training."

When you bring home your new Shih Tzu puppy, they will be relying upon your guidance to teach them what they need to learn, and when it comes to house training, the first thing the human guardian needs to learn is that the puppy is not being bad when they pee or poop inside.

They are just responding to the call of Mother Nature, and you need to pay close attention right from the very beginning, because it's entirely possible to teach a puppy to go to the bathroom outside in less than a week. Therefore, if your puppy is making bathroom "mistakes," blame yourself, not your puppy.

Check in with yourself and make sure your energy remains consistently calm and patient and that you exercise plenty of compassion and understanding while you help your new puppy learn the new bathroom rules.

Shih Tzu puppies and dogs flourish with routines and happily, so do humans, therefore, the first step is to establish a daily routine that will work efficiently for both canine and human alike.

While your puppy is still growing, on average, they can hold it approximately one hour for every month of their age. This means that if your 3-month-old puppy has been happily snoozing for two to three hours, as soon as they wake up, they will need to go outside.

Some of the first indications or signs that your puppy needs to be taken outside to relieve themselves will be when you see them:

• sniffing around
• circling
• looking for the door
• whining, crying, or barking
• acting agitated

Your happy praise will be a great help in quickly house training your puppy, because praise goes a long way toward encouraging and reinforcing future success when your Shih Tzu puppy makes the right decisions.

Also, during the early stages of potty training, adding treats as an extra incentive can be a good way to reinforce how happy you are that your puppy is learning to relieve themselves in the right place. Slowly, treats can be removed and replaced with your happy praise, or you can give your puppy a treat after they are back inside.

Next, now that you have a new puppy in your life, you will want to be flexible with respect to adapting your schedule to meet their internal clocks in order to quickly teach your Shih Tzu puppy their new bathroom routine.

This means not leaving your puppy alone for endless hours at a time, because firstly, they are pack animals that need companionship and your direction at all times, plus long periods alone will result in the disruption of the potty training schedule you have worked hard to establish.

If you have no choice but to leave your puppy alone for many hours, make sure that you place them in a paper-lined room or pen where they can relieve themselves without destroying your newly installed hardwood or favorite carpet.

Remember, your Shih Tzu is a growing puppy with a bladder and bowels that they do not yet have complete control over.

Bell Training

A very easy way to introduce your new Shih Tzu puppy to house training is to begin by teaching them how to ring a doorbell whenever they need to go outside.

Ringing a doorbell is not only a convenient alert system for both you and your Shih Tzu puppy or dog, your visitors will be most impressed by how smart your Shih Tzu is.

A further benefit of training your puppy to ring a bell is that you will not have to listen to your puppy or dog whining, barking, or howling to be let out, and your door will not become scratched up from their nails.

Attach the bell to a piece of ribbon or string and hang it from a door handle or tape it to a doorsill near the door where you will be taking your puppy out when they need to relieve themselves. The string will need to be long enough so that your Shih Tzu puppy can easily reach the bell with their nose or a paw.

Next, each time you take your puppy out to relieve themselves, say the word "Out," and use their paw or their nose to ring the bell. Praise them for this "trick" and immediately take them outside. This type of an alert system is an easy way to eliminate accidents in the home.

Kennel Training

When you train your Shih Tzu puppy to accept sleeping in their own kennel at nighttime, this will also help to accelerate their potty training, because no puppy or dog wants to relieve themselves where they sleep, which means that they will hold their bladder and bowels as long as they possibly can.

Presenting them with familiar scents by taking them to the same spot in the yard or the same street corner will help to remind and encourage them that they are outside to relieve themselves.

Use a voice cue to remind your puppy why they are outside, such as "go pee," and always remember to praise them every time they relieve themselves in the right place, so that they quickly understand what you expect of them and will learn to "go" on cue.

Exercise Pen Training

The exercise pen is a transition from kennel-only training and will be helpful for those times when you may have to leave your Shih Tzu puppy for more hours than they can reasonably be expected to hold it.

Exercise pens are usually constructed of wire sections that you can put together in whatever shape you desire, and the pen needs to be large enough to hold your puppy's kennel in one half of the pen, while the other half will be lined with newspapers or pee pads.

Place your Shih Tzu puppy's food and water dishes next to the kennel and leave the kennel door open (or take it off), so they can wander in and out whenever they wish, to eat or drink or go to the papers or pee pads if they need to relieve themselves.

Because they are already used to sleeping inside their kennel, they will not want to relieve themselves inside the area where they sleep. Therefore, your Shih Tzu puppy will naturally go to the other half of the pen to relieve themselves on the newspapers or pee pads.

Free Training

If you would rather not confine your young Shih Tzu puppy to one or two rooms in your home and will be allowing them to freely range about your home anywhere they wish during the day, this is considered free training.

When free house training your Shih Tzu puppy, you will need to closely watch your puppy's activities all day long so that you can be aware of the "signs" that will indicate when they need to go outside to relieve themselves.

Photo Credit: Susan Kilgore of Fantasy Shih Tzu

For instance, circling and sniffing is a sure sign that they are looking for a place to do their business.

Never get upset or scold a puppy for having an accident inside the home, because this will result in teaching your puppy to be afraid of you and to only relieve themselves in secret places or when you're not watching.

If you catch your Shih Tzu puppy making a mistake, all that is necessary is for you to calmly say "No" and quickly scoop them up and take them outside or to their indoor bathroom area.

From your puppy's point of view, yelling or screaming when they make a potty mistake is unstable energy being displayed by the person who is supposed to be their leader, and this type of behavior will only teach your puppy to fear and disrespect you.

The Shih Tzu is not a difficult puppy to housebreak, and they will generally do very well when you start them off with "puppy pee pads" that you will move closer and closer to the same door that you always use when taking them outside. This way, they will quickly learn to associate going to this door when they need to relieve themselves.

Your Shih Tzu puppy will always need to relieve themselves first thing in the morning, as soon as they wake up from a nap, approximately 20 minutes after they finish eating a meal, after they have finished a play session, and of course, before they go to bed at night.

Accidents DO Happen

Of course, nobody is perfect, and there will inevitably be little accidents during house training. There is no need to panic or worry excessively about this, so long as you are armed with the best cleaning products.

NOTE: a dog's sense of smell is at least 2,000 times more sensitive than our human sense of smell.

As a result of your Shih Tzu puppy's superior sense of smell, it will be very important to effectively remove all odors from house training accidents, because otherwise, your Shih Tzu puppy will be attracted by the smell and drawn to the place where they may have had a previous accident, and will want to do their business there again and again. This is not their fault.

While there are many products that are supposed to remove odors and stains, many of these are not very effective. You want a professional grade cleaner that will not just mask one odor with another scent, you want a product that will completely neutralize odors.

TIP: go to http://www.removeurineodors.com and order yourself some "SUN" and/or "Max Enzyme," because these products contain professional-strength odor neutralizers and urine digesters that bind to and completely absorb and eliminate odors on any type of surface, even that precious Persian carpet.

Chapter 5 - Socializing and Behavior

With Other Dogs and Pets

Generally speaking, the majority of an adult dog's habits and behavioral traits will be formed between the ages of birth and one year of age.

This is why it will be very important to introduce your Shih Tzu puppy to a wide variety and types of animals, locations, sights, sounds, and smells during this formative period in their young life.

Your Shih Tzu puppy will learn how to behave in all these various circumstances by following your lead, feeling your energy and watching how you react in every situation.

For instance, never accidentally reward your Shih Tzu puppy for displaying fear or growling at another dog or animal by picking them up.

Picking up a Shih Tzu puppy or dog at this time when they are displaying unbalanced energy actually turns out to be a reward for them, and you will be teaching them to continue with this type of behavior.

As well, picking up a puppy literally places them in a "top dog" position, where they are higher and more dominant than the dog or animal they just growled at.

The correct action to take in such a situation is to gently correct your Shih Tzu puppy with a firm, yet calm energy by distracting them with a "No," so that they learn to let you deal with the situation on their behalf.

If you allow a fearful or nervous puppy to deal with situations that unnerve them all by themselves, they may learn to react with fear or aggression, and you will have created a problem that could escalate into something quite serious as they grow older.

The same is true of situations where a young puppy may feel the need to protect themselves from a bigger or older dog that may come charging in for a sniff.

It is the guardian's responsibility to protect the puppy so that they do not think they must react with fear or aggression in order to protect themselves.

Once your Shih Tzu puppy has received all their vaccinations, you can take them out to public dog parks and various locations where many dogs are found.

Before allowing them to interact with other dogs or puppies, take them for a disciplined walk on leash so that they will be a little tired and less likely to immediately engage with all other dogs.

Keep your puppy on leash and close beside you, because most puppies are usually a bundle of out-of-control energy, and you need to protect them while teaching them how far they can go before getting themselves into trouble with adult dogs who may not appreciate excited puppy playfulness.

If your puppy shows any signs of aggression or domination toward another puppy or dog, you must immediately step in and calmly discipline them; by doing nothing, you will be allowing them to get into situations that could become serious behavioral issues.

With Other People

Take your puppy everywhere with you and introduce them to many different people of all ages, sizes, and ethnicities.

Most people will come to you and want to interact with your puppy. If they ask if they can hold your puppy, let them, because so long as they are gentle and don't drop the puppy, this is a good way to socialize your Shih Tzu and show them that humans are friendly.

Do not let others (especially children) play roughly with your puppy or squeal at them in high-pitched voices, because this can be very frightening for a young puppy. As well, you do not want to teach your puppy that humans are a source of excitement.

Be especially careful when introducing your puppy to young children who don't know how to act around a puppy and who may accidentally hurt your puppy, because you don't want them to become fearful of children, as this could lead to aggression later on in life.

Explain to children that your Shih Tzu puppy is very young and that they must be calm and gentle when playing or interacting in any way.

Within Different Environments

It can be a big mistake not to take the time to introduce your Shih Tzu puppy to a wide variety of different environments, because when they are not comfortable with different locations, sights and sounds, this could cause them possible trauma later in their adult life.

For instance, put your puppy in their Sherpa bag and take them to the airport where they can watch people and hear planes landing and taking off, take them to a park where they can see a baseball or soccer game, or take them to the local zoo or nearby farm and let them get a close up look at horses, pigs, chickens and ducks.

When you take your Shih Tzu puppy everywhere, you will be teaching them to be a calm and well-balanced member of your family in every situation.

Chapter 6 - Grooming and Care

Not taking the time to regularly involve your Shih Tzu puppy in grooming sessions could lead to serious, unwanted behavior that may include trauma to your dog, not to mention stress or injury to you in the form of biting and scratching.

When you neglect regular, daily, or at least a weekly at-home grooming session with your puppy or dog to remove tangles and keep mats to a minimum, it will also cost you a higher fee should you opt to have regular clipping and grooming carried out at a professional salon.

An effective home regimen will include not just surface brushing, but also getting to all those sensitive areas easily missed around the ears and collar area, the armpit area, and the back end and tail.

Do not allow yourself to get caught in the "my dog doesn't like it" trap, which is an excuse many owners will use to avoid regular grooming sessions. When you allow your dog to dictate whether they will permit a grooming session, you are setting a dangerous precedent.

Bath Time

Step One: before you get your Shih Tzu anywhere near the water, it's important to make sure that you brush out any debris, knots or tangles from their coat before you begin the bathing process, because getting knots or tangles wet could make them tighter and much more difficult to remove, which will cause your dog pain and distress.

As well, removing any debris from your dog's coat beforehand, including dead undercoat and shedding hair, will make the entire process easier on both you, your dog, and your drains, which will become clogged with hair if you don't remove it beforehand.

Step Two: if your Shih Tzu has a long coat, the process will be much easier if you first spray the coat with a light mist of leave-in conditioner before brushing. This will also help to protect the delicate hair strands from breaking.

Step Three: whether you're bathing your Shih Tzu in your kitchen sink, laundry tub or bathtub, you will always want to first lay down a rubber bath mat to provide a more secure footing for your dog and to prevent your sink or tub from being scratched.

Step Four: have everything you need for the bath (shampoo, conditioner, sponge, towels) right next to the sink or tub, so you don't have to go searching once your dog is already in the water.

TIP: place cotton balls in your Shih Tzu's ear canals to prevent accidental water splashes from entering the ear canal.

Step Five: fill the tub or sink with four to six inches of lukewarm water (not too hot as dogs are more sensitive to hot water than us humans) and put your Shih Tzu in the water. Completely wet your dog's coat right down to the skin by using a detachable shower head. If you don't have a spray attachment, a cup or pitcher will work just as well.

TIP: no dog likes to have water poured over their head and into its eyes, so use a wet sponge or wash cloth to wet the head area.

Step Six: apply shampoo as indicated on the bottle instructions by beginning at the head and working your way down the back. Be careful not to get shampoo in the eyes, nose, mouth or ears. Comb the shampoo lather through your dog's hair with your fingers, making sure you don't miss the areas under the legs and tail.

Step Seven: after allowing the shampoo to remain in your dog's coat for a couple of minutes, thoroughly rinse your Shih Tzu's coat right down to the skin with clean, lukewarm water using the spray attachment, cup or pitcher. Comb through your dog's coat with your fingers to make sure all shampoo residue has been rinsed away.

TIP: shampoo remaining in a dog's coat will lead to irritation and itching. Once you've rinsed, take the time to rinse again, especially in the armpits and underneath the tail area.

Use your hands to gently squeeze all excess water from your dog's coat.

Step Eight: apply conditioner as indicated on the bottle instructions and work the conditioner throughout your Shih Tzu's coat. Leave the conditioner in your dog's coat for two minutes and then thoroughly rinse the conditioner out with warm water, unless the conditioner you are using is a "leave-in," no-rinse formula.

Pull the plug on your sink or tub and let the water drain away as you use your hands to squeeze excess water from your Shih Tzu's legs and feet.

Step Nine: immediately out of the water, wrap your Shih Tzu in dry towels so they don't get cold, and use the towels to gently squeeze out extra water before you allow them a water-spraying shake. If your dog has long hair, do not rub your dog with the towels, as this will create tangles and breakage in the long hair.

NOTE: if your dog has a short or shaved coat, you will not need to be so particular, and in this case may massage the shampoo or conditioner in circular motions through the coat and can rub them down a little more with the towels after they are out of the tub.

Dry your Shih Tzu right away with your handheld hairdryer and be careful not to let the hot air get too close to their skin.

TIP: if your Shih Tzu's hair is longer, blow the hair in the direction of growth to help prevent breakage; if the hair is short, you can use your hand or a brush or comb to lift and fluff the hair to help it dry more quickly.

TIP: place your hand between the hairdryer and your Shih Tzu's hair so that they will never get a direct blast of hot air and never blow air directly into their face or ears.

Show Dog Coats

If you have decided to let your Shih Tzu keep a long, flowing coat that reaches the floor, be aware that this type of coat will be much higher maintenance.

Grooming can include weekly bathing and oiling of the coat to make the hair shine and to prevent hair from breaking, and at the very least, you will need to provide daily brushing and combing sessions to keep debris out of the longer hair.

Further, you will need to be much more careful when bathing a Shih Tzu with a long, silky coat.

For instance, when you apply the shampoo onto the back, you will not want to rub in circles, but rather use only downward strokes to distribute the suds, because washing up and down or massaging in circular motions will tangle and break the fine hair.

Clipping

If you have decided to learn how to clip your Shih Tzu's hair yourself, rather than taking them to a professional grooming salon, you will need to purchase all the tools necessary and learn how to properly use them.

The first step will be learning which blades to use in your electric clipper in order to get the length of cut you desire.

The "blade cut" refers to the length of the dog's hair that will remain after cutting against the natural lie of the hair.

As an example, if the blade cut indicates 1/4" (0.6 cm) the length of your Shih Tzu's hair after cutting will be 1/4" (0.6 cm) if you cut with the natural growth of their hair, or it will be 1/8" (0.3 cm) if you cut against the direction of the hair growth.

Even if you decide to leave the full grooming to the professionals, in between grooming sessions you will still need to have a brush, a comb, a small pair of scissors and a pair of nail clippers on hand, so that you can keep the hair clipped away from your Shih Tzu's eyes, knots and tangles out of their coat, and their nails trimmed short.

A good quality clipper for a Shih Tzu, such as an "Andis," "Wahl" or "Oster" professional electric clipper will cost between $100 and $300 (£60 and £180) or more, and blades cost extra.

Ear Care

There are many ear cleaning creams, drops, oils, rinses, solutions and wipes formulated for cleaning your dog's ears that you can purchase from your local pet store or veterinarian's office.

Or you may prefer to use a home remedy that will just as efficiently clean your Shih Tzu's ears, such as Witch Hazel or a 50:50 mixture of hydrogen peroxide and purified water.

TIP: if you are going to make your own ear cleaning solution, find a bottle with a nozzle, measure your solution, properly diluted and mixed into the bottle, and use your preparation to saturate a cotton makeup pad to wipe out the visible part of your dog's ears. Always make sure the ears are totally dried after cleaning.

Eye Care

Although some breeds, like the Shih Tzu, are much more prone to buildup of daily eye secretions, every dog should have their eyes regularly wiped with a warm, damp cloth to remove the buildup of secretions in the corners of the eyes.

The Shih Tzu will be prone to a buildup of secretions that can be unattractive and uncomfortable for the dog as the hair becomes glued together.

If this buildup is not removed every day, it can quickly become a cause of bacterial yeast growth that can lead to smelly eye infections.

When you take a moment every day to gently wipe your dog's eyes with a warm, moist cloth, and keep the hair trimmed away from their eyes, you will help to keep your dog's eyes comfortable and infection free.

Nail Care

Allowing your Shih Tzu to have long, untrimmed nails can result in various health hazards, including infections or an irregular and uncomfortable gait that can result in damage to their joints or skeleton.

Although most dogs do not particularly enjoy the process of having their nails trimmed, and most humans find the exercise to be a little scary, regular nail trimming is a very important grooming practice that should never be overlooked.

In order to keep your Shih Tzu's toenails in good condition and the proper length, you will need to purchase either a guillotine or plier-type nail trimmer at a pet store and learn how to correctly use it.

NOTE: when your Shih Tzu is a small puppy, it will be best to trim their nails with a pair of nail scissors, which you can purchase at any pet store, that are smaller and easier to use on smaller nails.

IMPORTANT NOTE: many dogs have dew claws that grow on the inside of their legs which never touch the ground. If you Shih Tzu has dew claws, remember to trim these too, otherwise they can get so long that they will grow around in a circle and actually penetrate the dog's leg, causing much pain and infection.

Further, if you want your dog's nails to be smooth, without the sharp edges clipping alone can create, you will also want to invest in a toenail file or a special, slow speed rotary trimmer (Dremel™) designed especially for dog nails. Some dogs will prefer the rotary trimmer to the squeezing sensation of the nail clipper.

NOTE: never use a regular Dremel™ tool, as it will be too high speed and will burn your dog's toenails. Only use a slow speed Dremel™, such as Model 7300-PT Pet Nail Grooming Tool (approx. $40/£20).

Dental Care

As a conscientious Shih Tzu guardian, you will need to regularly care for your dog's teeth throughout their entire life. This means, no excuses, being vigilant and brushing them every day!

Retained Primary Teeth

Often times a young dog will not naturally lose their puppy or baby teeth, especially those with small jaws, like the Shih Tzu, without intervention from a licensed veterinarian.

Therefore, keep a close watch on your puppy's teeth around the age of 6 or 7 months of age to make certain that the baby teeth have fallen out and that the adult teeth have space to grown in.

If your Shih Tzu puppy has not naturally lost some of their baby teeth, these will need to be pulled, in order to allow room for the adult teeth to grow in, and the best time to do this is when they visit the veterinarian's office to be spayed or neutered, because they will already be under anesthetic.

Smaller dogs, like the Shih Tzu, have a smaller jaw, which can result in more problems with teeth overcrowding.

An overcrowded mouth can cause teeth to grow unevenly or crooked and food and plaque to build up, which will eventually result in bacterial growth on the surface of the teeth, causing bad breath and gum and dental disease.

Periodontal Disease

Please be aware that 80% of three-year-old dogs suffer from periodontal disease and bad breath because their guardians do not look after their dog's teeth.

What makes this shocking statistic even worse is that it is entirely possible to prevent canine gum disease and bad breath.

The pain associated with periodontal disease will make your dog's life miserable, as it will be painful for them to eat and the associated bacteria can infect many parts of the dog's body, including the heart, kidney, liver and brain, all of which they will have to suffer in silence.

Bad breath could be the first sign of gum disease caused by plaque buildup on the teeth. Plaque changes the color of the teeth, making them brown or gray, and it can quickly build up with a consistency of cement on the surface of the back teeth, while pushing up the gums.

As well, if your Shih Tzu is drooling excessively, this may be a symptom secondary to dental disease. Your dog may be experiencing pain, or the salivary glands may be reacting to inflammation from excessive bacteria in the mouth.

Teeth Brushing

Slowly introduce your Shih Tzu to teeth brushing early on in their young life so that they will not fear it.

Begin with a finger cap toothbrush when they are young puppies, and then move to a soft bristled toothbrush, and then graduate to an electric brush, as all you have to do is hold it against the teeth while the brush does all the work. Sometimes with a manual brush, you may brush too hard and cause the gums to bleed.

Never use human toothpaste or mouthwash on your dog's teeth, because dogs cannot spit, and human toothpaste that contains toxic fluoride will be swallowed. There are many flavored dog toothpastes available at the pet store or veterinarian's office.

Also, it's a good idea to get your dog used to the idea of occasionally having their teeth scraped or scaled, especially the back molars, which tend to build up plaque.

TIP: if you need help keeping your dog's mouth open while you do a quick brush or scrape, get yourself a piece of hard material (rubber or leather) that they can bite down on, so that they cannot fully close their mouth while you work on their teeth. It helps greatly to have an assistant hold your dog while you work on their teeth.

Next, buy some canine toothpaste at your local pet store specially flavored to appeal to dogs and apply this to your dog's teeth with your finger.

Then slowly introduce the manual or electric toothbrush to your Shih Tzu. When you go slowly, they will get used to the buzzing of the electric brush which will do a superior job of cleaning their teeth.

First, let them see the electric brush, then let them hear it buzzing, and before you put it in their mouth, let them feel the buzzing sensation on their body, while you move it slowly toward their head and muzzle.

When your Shih Tzu will allow you to touch their muzzle while the brush is turned on, the next step is to brush a couple of teeth at a time until they get used to having them all brushed at the same time.

Make certain that you brush in a circular motion with the bristles of the brush angled so that they get underneath the gum line to help prevent plaque buildup that leads to gum disease and loose teeth.

Healthy Teeth Tips

Despite what most dog owners might put up with as normal, it is not normal for your dog to have smelly dog breath or canine halitosis.

Bad breath is the first sign of an unhealthy mouth, which could involve gum disease or tooth decay.

The following tips will help keep your Shih Tzu's mouth and teeth healthy:

1. Keep your dog's teeth sparkling white and their breath fresh by using old-fashioned hydrogen peroxide as your doggy toothpaste (hydrogen peroxide is what's in the human whitening toothpaste). There will be such a small amount on the brush that it will not harm your dog and will kill any bacteria in your dog's mouth. Give the roof of their mouth a quick brush, too.

2. Many canine toothpastes are formulated with active enzymes to help keep tartar buildup at bay.

3. Help prevent tooth plaque and doggy halitosis by feeding your dog natural, hard bones at least once a month, which will also help to remove tartar while polishing and keeping their teeth white. Feed large bones so there is no danger of swallowing, and do NOT boil the bones first, because this makes the bone soft (which defeats the purpose of removing plaque) and may cause it to splinter into smaller pieces that could create a choking hazard for your dog.

4. Small dogs with shorter muzzles, such as the Shih Tzu, tend to be more vulnerable to teeth and gum problems, therefore, you really need to be brushing their teeth every single day.

5. Feed a daily dental chew or hard biscuit to help remove tartar while exercising jaws and massaging

gums. Some dental chews contain natural breath freshening cinnamon, cloves or chlorophyll.

6. Coconut oil also helps to prevent smelly dog breath while giving your dog's digestive, immune and metabolic functions a boost at the same time. Dogs love the taste, so add a 1/2 tsp to your Shih Tzu's dinner, and their breath will soon be much sweeter.

7. Keep your Shih Tzu's mouth comfortable and healthy by getting into the habit of brushing their teeth every night before bedtime.

Skin Care

Keeping your Shih Tzu's coat clean by regularly bathing with canine shampoo and conditioner and free from debris and parasites, as well as providing plenty of clean water and feeding them a high quality diet free from allergy-causing ingredients, will go a long way toward keeping their skin healthy and itch free.

Brushing and Combing

Brushing and combing your dog's coat is an often-overlooked task that is a necessary part of maintaining your dog's health.

As well, taking time to brush and comb your Shih Tzu's coat will give you an opportunity to bond with your dog, while identifying any problems (such as lumps or bumps and matted hair), ticks or fleas early on, before they become more serious.

Make sure that your grooming sessions are as pleasant as possible by choosing the right tools for a Shih Tzu and their type and length of coat.

You will need a variety of brushes and combs to keep your Shih Tzu's coat in good condition; these will include a soft bristle brush, a slicker brush, and a pin brush.

As well as your collection of brushes, you will need to invest in a metal comb, a flea comb and perhaps a mat splitter.

Equipment and Supplies Required

A bristle brush with its clusters of tightly packed bristles will remove loose hair, dirt and debris while gently stimulating the skin, improving circulation and adding shine to the coat.

A pin brush usually has an oval head with wire bristles that are individually spaced and embedded into a flexible rubber pad.

Most guardians prefer pin brushes with rubber tips as these help to prevent a wire from accidentally piercing a dog's sensitive skin.

A pin brush is more normally used following a thorough bristle brushing to lift and fluff the hair at the end of a grooming session.

A slicker brush has short, thin, wire bristles arranged closely together and anchored to a flat, often rectangular surface that's attached to a handle.

A slicker brush is an ideal grooming tool for helping to remove mats and tangles from a Shih Tzu's coat. Slicker brushes are often used as a finishing brush after the use of a pin brush to smooth the dog's coat and create a shiny finish.

Mat Splitters, as the name suggests, are tools for splitting apart matted hair, and they come in three different types, including the letter opener style, the safety razor style, and the curved blade style.

All of these tools are used to split matted fur into smaller, lengthwise pieces, with minimal discomfort to the dog, so that you or your groomer can untangle or shave the area with a clipper.

Combs are very useful for getting down to the base of any tangles in a dog's coat and working them loose before they develop into painful mats.

Most metal combs have a combination of widely spaced and narrowly spaced teeth and are designed so that if you run into a tangle, you can switch to the wider spaced teeth while you work it out without pulling and irritating your dog.

NOTE: Some combs have rotating teeth, which makes the process of removing tangles from your Shih Tzu's coat much easier on them without the pain of pulling and snagging.

Flea combs, as the name suggests, are designed for the specific purpose of removing fleas from a dog's coat.

A flea comb is usually small in size for maneuvering in tight spaces, and may be made of plastic or metal with the teeth of the comb very close together, to trap hiding fleas.

As well, you will want to keep a good quality pair of small scissors in your Shih Tzu grooming box, even if you do not want to do the full grooming process yourself, so that you can regularly trim around your Shih Tzu's eyes between full grooming sessions.

If you are planning to groom your Shih Tzu yourself, you will need to invest in good quality scissors of several lengths that can cost anywhere between $30 and $200 each (£18 and £119) or more.

Products

Shampoos

NEVER make the mistake of using human shampoo or conditioner for bathing your Shih Tzu, because dogs have a different pH balance than humans.

For example, shampoo for humans has a pH balance of 5.5, whereas shampoo formulated for our canine companions has an almost neutral pH balance of 7.5.

Any shampoo with a lower pH balance will be harmful to your dog because it will be too harshly acidic for their coat and skin, which can create skin problems.

Always purchase a shampoo for your dog that is specially formulated to be gentle and moisturizing on your Shih Tzu's coat and skin, will not strip the natural oils, and will nourish your dog's coat to give it a healthy shine.

As a general rule, always read the instructions provided on the shampoo bottle and avoid shampoos containing insecticides or harsh chemicals.

TIP: if your Shih Tzu is suffering from an infestation of fleas, you may want to bathe them with shampoo containing pyrethrum (a botanical extract found in small, white daisies) or a shampoo containing citrus oil.

Conditioners

While many of us humans use a conditioner after we shampoo our own hair, a large number of us canine guardians forget to use a conditioner on our own dog's coat after bathing.

Conditioning your Shih Tzu's coat will not only make it look and feel better, conditioning will also add additional benefits, including:

- preventing the escape of natural oils and moisture;
- keeping the coat cleaner for a longer period of time;
- repairing a coat that has become damaged or dry;

- restoring a soft, silky feel;
- making the coat shine;
- helping the coat dry more quickly;
- protecting from the heat of the dryer and breakage from tangles during toweling, combing or brushing.

Spend the extra two minutes to condition your Shih Tzu's coat after bathing, because the benefits of doing so will be appreciated by both you and your dog, who will have an overall healthy coat and skin with a natural shine.

De-tanglers

There are many de-tangling products you can purchase that will make the job of combing and removing mats much easier on both you and your Shih Tzu, especially if you have opted to let their hair grow longer.

De-tangling products work by making the hair slippery, and while some de-tanglers work well when used full strength, you may prefer a lighter, spray-in product.

As well, there are silicone products and grooming powders, or you can use corn starch to effectively lubricate the hair to help with removing mats and tangles before bathing.

Styptic Powder

You will always want to avoid causing any pain when trimming your Shih Tzu's toenails, because you don't want to destroy their trust in you regularly performing this task.

However, accidents do happen, therefore if you accidentally cut into the vein in the toenail, know that you will cause your dog pain, and that the toenail will bleed.

Keep some styptic powder (often called "Kwik Stop") in your grooming kit in case you accidentally cut a nail too short. Dip a moistened finger into the powder and apply it immediately to the end of the bleeding nail.

The quickest way to stop a nail from bleeding is to immediately apply styptic powder and firm pressure for a few seconds.

TIP: if you do not have styptic powder or a styptic pencil available, there are several home remedies that can help stop the bleeding, including a mixture of baking soda and corn starch, or simply corn starch alone.

Also, a cold, wet teabag or rubbing with scent-free soap can also be effective. These home remedies will not be as instantly effective as styptic powder.

Ear Powders

Ear powders, which can be purchased at any pet store, are designed to help keep your dog's ears dry while at the same time inhibiting the growth of bacteria that can lead to infections. You may want to apply a little ear powder after washing the inside of your dog's ears to help ensure that they are totally dry.

Ear Cleaning Solutions

Your local pet store will offer a wide variety of ear cleaning creams, drops, oils, rinses, solutions, and wipes specially formulated for cleaning your dog's ears.

NOTE: because a dog's ears are a very sensitive area, always read the labels before purchasing products and avoid any solutions that list alcohol as the main ingredient.

Home Ear Cleaning Solutions

The following are three effective home solutions that will efficiently clean your dog's ears:

Witch Hazel is a natural anti-inflammatory that works well to cleanse and protect against infection while encouraging faster healing of minor skin traumas.

A 50:50 solution of organic apple cider vinegar and purified water has been used as an external folk medicine for decades. This mixture is a gentle and effective solution that kills germs while naturally healing.

A 50:50 solution of hydrogen peroxide and purified water is useful for cleansing wounds and dissolving ear wax.

Whatever product you decide to use for cleaning your dog's ears, always be careful about what you put into the ears and thoroughly dry them after cleaning.

Paw Creams

Depending upon the types of surfaces our canine counterparts usually walk on and whether you live in a dry or hot climate, they may suffer from cracked or rough pads.

You can restore resiliency and keep your Shih Tzu's paws in healthy condition by regularly applying a cream or lotion to protect their paw pads.

TIP: a good time to do this is just after you have clipped their nails.

Professional Grooming

If you decide that you are not interesting in buying all the equipment (electric clippers, blades, scissors, nail clippers, combs, brushes, table, etc.) or enrolling yourself in a $4,000 (£2,388) course to learn how to professionally groom your Shih Tzu yourself, you will want to locate a trusted professional service to do this for you.

If you have decided to keep your Shih Tzu clipped short, you will need to take them for a full grooming session approximately every 6 to 8 weeks.

An average price for professionally grooming a small Shih Tzu will usually start around $40 (£24) and could be considerably more depending upon whether the salon is also bathing and trimming nails.

Chapter 7 - Health

Medical Care - Choosing a Veterinarian

While choosing a clinic will be a personal decision, since the Shih Tzu is considered a small or "toy" breed of dog, your dog's needs may be better served by choosing a clinic that specializes in caring for the health needs of smaller pets.

Of course, you will want to ensure that your Shih Tzu puppy receives the quality care they deserve, and the best way to accomplish this will be to begin your search by asking your family, friends, neighbors and other fellow dog guardians you may meet where they take their furry companions and how satisfied they are.

If you are new to the area and don't know anyone to ask, search out your local pet store or a professional grooming business in your area who should be able to provide you with opinions and suggest local veterinarian services.

Once you've narrowed your search, it's time to take yourself and your new little Shih Tzu puppy for a personal visit. This will be a good opportunity for you to visually inspect the facility, interact with the staff and perhaps meet the veterinarians face to face. This will give you a feeling for their experience and expertise in handling your puppy.

You will also want to take your puppy into your chosen clinic several times before they actually need to be there, so that they are not fearful of the new smells and unfamiliar surroundings.

Under the Knife

Different people will offer different answers when asked, "When is the best time to neuter or spay my puppy?" However, most veterinarians do agree that earlier (rather than later) spaying or neutering, between 4 and 6 months of age, is a better choice. This advice however is challenged in the United Kingdom, where many breeders have told me they believe a puppy should be left to settle and reach maturity before the operation is carried out.

Effects on Aggression

It's an indisputable fact that sterilized males and females are more likely to display less aggression related to sexual behavior than puppies that are not neutered or spayed. Fighting between males is less common after neutering.

The intensity of other types of aggression, such as irritable aggression in females, who may growl and snap at every other dog in the vicinity, will be totally eliminated by spaying.

While neutering or spaying is not a treatment for aggression, it can certainly help to minimize the severity of aggressiveness and is often the first step taken toward resolving an aggressive behavior problem.

What is Neutering and Spaying?

Neutering and spaying are surgical procedures carried out by your licensed veterinary surgeon, under local anesthetic, to prevent unwanted pregnancies.

The simple surgery carried out on male puppies that makes most male humans squeamish (castration) involves removing the young dog's testicles. When this procedure is carried out, what's left behind is an empty scrotal sac which will quickly shrink in size until it is no longer noticeable.

Neutering a male puppy before they are six months of age provides several benefits, including that they will:

• be less likely to suffer from obesity as they mature
• be less likely to have the urge to wander
• not have to experience raging mating hormones

• not feel the need to spray or mark territory to attract mates
• be less likely to display aggression toward other males

Spaying a female puppy is a more involved surgical procedure, as it requires the removal of both ovaries by incision into the puppy's abdominal cavity. The uterus is also removed during this surgery to prevent the possibility of it becoming infected later on in life.

Spaying a female puppy before they are six months of age provides several benefits, including:

• not having to experience their first estrus or heat cycle
• eliminating the hormonal stress of heat cycles
• eliminating hormonal aggression toward other dogs
• reducing the possibility of mammary gland infection.
• protection against uterine infections

Improved Temperament

Many dog guardians become needlessly worried that a neutered or spayed dog will lose their vigor or joy of life.

Not to worry, because a young dog's personality or energy level will not be modified by neutering or spaying, and in fact, many unfavorable qualities that are a direct result of raging hormones may completely resolve after surgery.

Your Shih Tzu will certainly not hold a grudge or come to be less caring or cheerful, and neither will it resent you because it was denied mating encounters.

Further, while old wives tales abound, there is no concrete evidence to suggest that the nature of a female Shih Tzu will improve after having a litter of puppies.

What is important here is that you do not project your own psychological needs or concerns onto your Shih Tzu puppy, because there is no gain to be had from permitting sexual activity in either male or female canines.

When Is a Puppy Vaccinated?

The first vaccination needle is normally given to a puppy around the age of six to eight weeks, which means that usually it will be the responsibility of the Shih Tzu breeder to ensure that the puppy's first shots have been received before their new owner takes them home.

Then it will be the new Shih Tzu puppy's guardians that will be responsible for ensuring that the next two sets of shots, which are given three to four weeks after each other, are administered by the new guardian's veterinarian at the proper intervals.

DAPP Vaccinations

All puppies are vaccinated by a licensed veterinarian in order to provide them with protection against the four most common and serious diseases, which include Distemper, Adenovirus, Parainfluenza and Parvovirus. This set of four primary vaccinations is referred to as "DAPP."

Approximately one week after your Shih Tzu puppy has completed all three sets of DAPP vaccinations, they will be fully protected from these four specific diseases. Then, most veterinarians will recommend a once-a-year vaccination for the next year or two.

NOTE: it has now become common practice to vaccinate adult dogs every three years, and if your veterinarian is insisting on a yearly vaccination for your Shih Tzu puppy after they have had their second birthday, you need to ask them why, because to do otherwise is considered by most professionals to be "over vaccinating."

Distemper

Canine distemper is a contagious and serious viral illness for which there is currently no known cure.

This deadly virus, which is spread either through the air or by direct or indirect contact with a dog that is already infected, or other distemper carrying wildlife, including ferrets, raccoons, foxes, skunks and wolves, is a relative of the measles virus that affects humans.

Canine distemper is sometimes also called "hard pad disease" because some strains of the distemper virus actually cause thickening of the pads on a dog's feet, which can also affect the end of a dog's nose.

In dogs or animals with weak immune systems, death may result two to five weeks after the initial infection.

Early symptoms of distemper include fever, loss of appetite, and mild eye inflammation that may only last a day or two. Symptoms become more serious and noticeable as the disease progresses.

A puppy or dog that survives the distemper virus will usually continue to experience symptoms or signs of the disease throughout their remaining lifespan, including "hard pad disease" as well as "enamel hypoplasia," which is damage to the enamel of the puppy's teeth that are not yet formed or that have not yet pushed through the gums.

Enamel hypoplasia is caused by the distemper virus killing the cells that manufacture tooth enamel.

Adenovirus

This virus causes infectious canine hepatitis, which can range in severity from very mild to very serious or even cause death.

Symptoms can include coughing, loss of appetite, increased thirst and urination, tiredness, runny eyes and nose, vomiting, bruising or bleeding under the skin, swelling of the head, neck and trunk, fluid accumulation in the abdomen area, jaundice (yellow tinge to the skin), a bluish clouding of the cornea of the eye (called "hepatitis blue eye") and seizures.

There is no specific treatment for infectious canine hepatitis, and treatment is focused on managing symptoms while the virus runs its course. Hospitalization and intravenous fluid therapy may be required in severe cases.

Parainfluenza Virus

The canine parainfluenza virus originally affected only horses but has now adapted to become contagious to dogs. Also referred to as "canine influenza virus," "greyhound disease" or "race flu," it is easily spread from dog to dog through the air or by coming into contact with respiratory secretions from an infected animal.

While the more frequent occurrences of this respiratory infection are seen in areas with high dog populations, such as race tracks, boarding kennels and pet stores, this virus is highly contagious to any dog or puppy, regardless of age.

Symptoms can include a dry, hacking cough, difficulty breathing, wheezing, runny nose and eyes, sneezing, fever, loss of appetite, tiredness, depression and possible pneumonia.

In cases where only a cough exists, tests will be required to determine whether the cause of the cough is the parainfluenza virus or the less serious "kennel cough."

While many dogs can naturally recover from this virus, they will remain contagious, and for this reason, in order to prevent the spread to other animals, aggressive treatment of the virus with antibiotics and antiviral drugs will be the prescribed course of action.

In more severe cases, a cough suppressant may be used, as well as intravenous fluids to help prevent secondary bacterial infection.

Parvovirus

Canine parvovirus is a highly contagious viral illness affecting puppies and dogs that also affects other canine species, including foxes, coyotes and wolves.

There are two forms of this virus — (1) the more common intestinal form and (2) the less common cardiac form, which can cause death in young puppies.

Symptoms of the intestinal form of parvovirus include vomiting, bloody diarrhea, weight loss and lack of appetite, while the less common cardiac form attacks the heart muscle.

Early vaccination in young puppies has radically reduced the incidence of canine parvovirus infection, which is easily transmitted either by direct contact with an infected dog, or indirectly, by sniffing an infected dog's feces.

The virus can also be brought into a dog's environment on the bottom of human shoes that may have stepped on infected feces, and there is evidence that this hardy virus can live in ground soil for up to a year.

Recovery from parvovirus requires both aggressive and early treatment. With proper treatment, death rates are relatively low (between 5 and 20%), although chances of survival for puppies are much lower than older dogs, and in all instances, there is no guarantee of survival.

Treatment of parvovirus requires hospitalization where intravenous fluids and nutrients are administered to help combat dehydration. As well, antibiotics will be given to counteract secondary bacterial infections, and as necessary, medications to control nausea and vomiting may be given.

Without prompt and proper treatment, dogs that have severe parvovirus infections can die within 48 to 72 hours.

Rabies Vaccinations

Rabies is a viral disease transmitted through the saliva of an infected animal, usually through a bite.

The virus travels to the brain along the nerves, and once symptoms develop, death is almost certainly inevitable, usually following a prolonged period of suffering.

Leishmaniasis

Leishmaniasis is caused by a parasite and is transmitted by a bite from a sand fly. There is no definitive answer for effectively combating leishmaniasis, especially since one vaccine will not prevent the known multiple species.

NOTE: Leishmaniasis is a "zoonotic" infection, which means that this is a contagious disease, and that organisms residing in the Leishmaniasis lesions can be spread between animals and humans and ultimately communicated to humans.

Lyme Disease

This is one of the most common tick-borne diseases in the world, which is transmitted by Borrelia bacteria found in the deer or sheep tick.

Lyme disease, also called "borreliosis," can affect both humans and dogs and can be fatal.

There is a vaccine for Lyme disease, and dogs living in areas that have easy access to these ticks should be vaccinated yearly.

Rocky Mountain Spotted Fever

This tick-transmitted disease is very often seen in dogs in the east, Midwest, and plains regions of the U.S., and the organisms causing Rocky Mountain Spotted Fever (RMSF) are transmitted by both the American dog tick and the RMSF tick, which must be attached to the dog for a minimum of five hours in order to transmit the disease.

Ehrlichiosis

This is another tick disease transmitted by both the brown dog tick and the lone star tick.

Ehrlichiosis has been reported in every state in the U.S., as well as worldwide. There is no vaccine available.

Anaplasmosis

Deer ticks and western black-legged ticks are carriers of the bacteria that transmit canine anaplasmosis.

However, there is another form of anaplasmosis that is carried by the brown dog tick. Because the deer tick also carries other diseases, some animals may be at risk for developing more than one tick-borne disease at the same time.

Tick Paralysis

Tick paralysis is caused when ticks secrete a toxin that affects the nervous system.

Affected dogs show signs of weakness and limpness approximately one week after being first bitten by ticks, and treatment involves locating and removing the tick and then treating with tick anti-serum.

Canine Coronavirus

This highly contagious intestinal disease is spread through the feces of contaminated dogs and was first discovered in Germany during 1971 when there was an outbreak in sentry dogs; it is now found worldwide.

This virus can be destroyed by most commonly available disinfectants, and there is a vaccine available that is usually given to puppies that are more susceptible at a young age and to show dogs that have a higher risk of exposure to the disease.

Leptosporosis

This is a disease that occurs throughout the World that can affect many different kinds of animals, including dogs, because it is found in rats and other wildlife as well as domestic livestock.

While dogs usually become infected by sniffing infected urine or by wading, swimming in or drinking contaminated water (this is how the disease passes from animal to animal), the leptospira can also enter through a bite wound or by dogs eating infected material.

Depending upon where you and your Shih Tzu live, and whether you plan to travel to different countries, your veterinarian may suggest additional vaccinations to help combat diseases that may be more common in your area or in areas you plan to visit.

De-worming

De-worming kills internal parasites that your dog or puppy has, and no matter where you live, how sanitary your conditions, or how much of a neat freak you are, your dog will have internal parasites, because it is not a matter of cleanliness.

It is recommended by the Centers for Disease Control and Prevention (CDC) that puppies be de-wormed every 2 weeks until they are 3 months old, and then every month after that in order to control worms.

Many veterinarians recommend worming dogs for tapeworm and roundworms every 6-12 months.

While de-worming kills most internal parasites, your vet may prescribe different treatments for giardia and coccidiosis. Be sure to have your dog's stool samples checked for worms as well as other parasites as mentioned.

Licensing

Our fur friends are required to be licensed in many cities and jurisdictions around the world.

In most cases, a dog license will be a light metal tag that the dog will be required to wear on their collar. The tag will be inscribed with an identifying number as well as a contact number for the registering organization, so that a lost dog found wearing a tag can be easily reunited with its guardian.

Most dog tags or licenses need to be renewed each year, which involves paying, in most cases, a reasonable fee.

Of course, where you and your dog reside may have a huge impact on how much, or any, fees you are required to pay.

Using both ends of the licensing scale as an example, owners of dogs living in Beijing, China must pay a licensing fee of $600 (£360), while dogs living in Great Britain are no longer required to be licensed at all, because licensing requirements were abolished in 1987.

Ireland requires dogs to be licensed, and in Germany dog ownership is taxed rather than requiring licensing, with higher taxes being paid for breeds of dogs deemed to be "dangerous."

Many other parts of the world have reasonable licensing fees for our fur friends.

For instance, U.S. states and municipalities have licensing laws in effect, and Canadian, Australian and New Zealand dogs also must be licensed, with the yearly cost between $30 and $50 (£18 to £30).

Fees are often less if the dog is spayed or neutered, and some municipalities offer the first dog tag free with proof of a neutering or spaying certificate from your veterinarian.

Pet Insurance

In light of all the new treatments and medications that are now available for our canine companions, which usually come with a very high price tag, an increasing number of guardians have decided to add pet insurance to their list of essential monthly expenses.

On the other hand, some humans believe that setting funds aside in a savings account, as a buffer for unforeseen medical expenses, makes more sense.

Over the average lifetime of a beloved fur friend, pet insurance coverage could cost anywhere from $2,000 to $6,000 USD (£1201 to £3604), and unless your dog is involved in a serious accident, you may never need to pay out that much for treatment.

For those humans who may not yet be independently wealthy, pet insurance can certainly provide peace of mind that could be much easier to take than the extra stress involved in going into debt should you be faced with a costly veterinarian bill.

Veterinary science has advanced considerably in recent years, which means that our canine companions now have access to sophisticated diagnostic equipment, so long as you can pay for it.

Our dogs are now being offered treatment options that were once only reserved for humans, and some canine conditions that were once considered fatal are being treated at considerable costs ranging anywhere from $1,000 to $5,000 (£597 to £2,986) — or more!

Interestingly, even in the face of rapidly increasing costs of caring for our dogs, owners purchasing pet insurance still remain a small minority.

Shop around, because as with all insurance policies, pet insurance policies will vary greatly between companies.

Read the fine print because there are many policies containing small print that excludes certain ages and hereditary or chronic conditions.

There are several questions to ask an insurance provider before choosing a pet insurance policy, including:
- Is your dog required to undergo a physical exam?
- Is there a waiting period before the policy starts?
- What percentage of the bill does the insurance company pay — after the deductible?
- Are payments limited or capped in any way?
- Are there co-pays (costs to you up front)?
- Does the plan cover pre-existing conditions?
- Are chronic or recurring medical problems covered?
- Are fees higher depending on the breed of dog?
- Can you choose any veterinarian or animal hospital?
- Are prescription medications covered?
- Are you covered when traveling with your pet?

The right pet insurance policy can provide both peace of mind and better health care for your beloved fur friend.

Protective Eyewear

Doggles™ are functional, fashionable, protective eye protection for all sizes of dogs.

Getting your dog used to wearing this protective eyewear at a young age is a really good idea for any Shih Tzu to help prevent some of the more common eye problems, especially those caused by dirt, pollen and other debris in the air, wind or glare from the sunshine.

As well, when you get your Shih Tzu used to wearing Doggles™, you will help to prevent your fur friend getting cataracts from too much exposure to sunlight.

Keep them on for short periods only until they get used to wearing them for longer periods of time without fussing, and soon they will accept them without fuss.

http://www.doggles.com

Travel Safety

Far too many canine guardians do absolutely nothing to protect their canine companions when traveling with them in their vehicles.

According to a 2011 American Automobile Association study, less than 20% of dog owners restrain their pets when riding in a vehicle, and of those who are trying, many are missing the mark.

Could you ever forgive yourself if you were the cause of your dog's death?

By far, the easiest and safest travel arrangement for any dog is to secure them inside a travel bag or kennel that is already tied down by the vehicle's restraint system, followed by finding a safety restraint that is crash and strength tested and certified to be safe for your dog.

Harness Restraints

The Kurgo Tru-Fit Smart Harness has been crash and strength tested, and with its steel nesting buckles has the tensile strength to withstand a force of 2,250 pounds (1,020 kilogram-force).

The Ruff Rider Roadie® harness successfully passed the preliminary test criteria for both dynamic and static load limits. Ruff Rider's product, the Roadie® travel restraint, was invented by dog owner Carl Goldberg after his pet was ejected through the front windshield in a collision.

Sherpa for Small Dogs

The Sherpa is a name that refers to a soft-sided dog carrier with zippered pockets for carrying important papers, treats, baggies, etc. that has mesh sides for superior ventilation.

While there is an actual "Sherpa" brand name, "Sherpa" has become synonymous with any type of soft-sided carrier bag for dogs.

The bag has handles as well as a shoulder strap and some even have wheels, so your Shih Tzu puppy or dog will be able to safely travel anywhere with you in style and comfort, so long as you get them used to the idea when they are a young puppy.

When they are young puppies, put them inside their bag every time they need to go outside and before you bring them back inside. When you do this, a Shih Tzu puppy will very quickly learn to love scooting into their bag, because they associate it with the fun activity of going outside.

There is one manufacturer of a travel bag restraint system called "Sleepypod™," designed for pets up to 15 pounds (6.8 kg), that goes the extra mile for safety and actually puts its own products through the child safety seat test. All four models of the Sleepypod™ have passed the 30 mph (48.28 km/h) crash test.

http://www.sleepypod.com

Although these bags are considerably more costly than many other canine travel bags or Sherpas, you will have peace of mind knowing that your little Shih Tzu will always be safe when riding inside one.

Common Problems

The most common issues seen with Shih Tzus are breathing, eye, ear and dental health problems and some back problems.

Breathing Problems

While not every short-faced or brachycephalic dog will develop respiratory problems, most will display common symptoms, such as "reverse sneezing," to some degree.

In severe cases, surgery is recommended, which involves applying prosthetic rings to the outside of the trachea.

Reverse sneezing is a phenomenon of the breed that can be very startling to the Shih Tzu guardian when they hear this snorting, gagging or honking sound for the first time.

Often it is brought on when a dog becomes overly excited from quickly eating special treats, or when greeting another dog or friend. Usually the dog will stop moving and hang its head during a reverse sneezing episode, and although it may be distressing to the dog, it is usually more distressing to the Shih Tzu owner.

There are several methods that can help a dog overcome a reverse sneezing episode, including calming them, rubbing their nose so that they open their mouth and begin breathing normally, and giving their chest a quick little squeeze on either side to force air out of their lungs. Sometimes, lightly blowing air into their face will also relieve the episode.

Most dogs will appear completely normal both before and after episodes of reverse sneezing and will continue to experience them intermittently throughout their lives.

Dogs that have severe respiratory disorders may have increasingly noisy breathing, coughing, gagging, fainting or collapsing episodes from lack of oxygen, and in these cases, over the long term, without surgical intervention, there will be an increased strain on the heart.

Overheating can be a serious problem for dogs suffering from severe respiratory problems, because the increased panting causes further swelling and narrowing of the airways, so if your dog has a severe breathing problem, it will be advisable not to exercise them in hot weather.

Eye Problems

The Shih Tzu has a short nose or face and large eyes with shallow eye sockets, which can result in several eye problems, including:

Infections: foreign materials are always floating or flying about in the air, and when they enter the eye area, they can cause inflammation and infection.

Corneal Ulcers: while all Shih Tzu eyes are not the same, those with more protruding eyes can be at greater risk for corneal ulcers, which are caused by wind blowing against the eyes or foreign objects scratching the eye.

Cataracts: many dogs will experience cataracts as they age, and this condition may be more prevalent in the Shih Tzu breed because their eyes generally tend to be more protruded. When cataracts develop, a Shih Tzu will lose vision in that eye, and if the condition affects both eyes, it can lead to blindness.

Entropion: is a condition whereby one or both of the Shih Tzu eyelids turns inward, causing the eyelashes to irritate the eyeball. It can be corrected with surgery.

Epiphoria: is also referred to as "wet eye," which is an overflowing of tears or excessive tearing that can occur when a dog's tear ducts do not drain properly. Epiphoria is generally a result of the Shih Tzu's short face. Infections and other eye issues can also cause this condition.

Distichiasis: is a condition where the eyelashes are located within the eye lid margin. This can cause a scratching of the cornea and much irritation. Treatment is to remove the eyelashes via epilation, electro-epilation, cyrotherapy or surgical excision.

Dry Eye: is a condition where not enough of the watery portion of tearing is produced. Otherwise known as keratoconjuctivitis sicca (KCS), artifical tears, cyclosporine and/or antibiotics may be the prescribed by your vet.

Cherry Eye: is an inherited condition that is seen as the enlargement of the nictitans gland, not to be confused with the blockage and thus swelling from an infection of the inner duct glands. Treatment of an enlarged may require surgery for correction or complete removal of the gland. Treatment of the infected inner duct glands includes the application of a warm compress with slight pressure to soothe the infected glands, followed with an antibiotic eye ointment.

Back Problems

As a result of the Shih Tzu body generally being slightly longer than it is tall, they can suffer from back and neck problems that may result in a condition called "intervertebral disk disease."

The intervertebral disks function to cushion the spine, and if they bulge or rupture, can cause nerve problems as well as loss of coordination and severe pain. Without treatment it can result in permanent weakness or paralysis.

Teeth Problems

All dogs require teeth care. Dogs with small jaws require special teeth care, and this means the Shih Tzu, too.

Without proper daily dental care, your adult Shih Tzu could suffer terribly and die prematurely. This topic was discussed in more detail in chapter six.

Ear Problems

Ear infections (otitis externa) can be common in any breed, but especially in flop-eared breeds like the Shih Tzu, whose ears hang as opposed to being held erect.

An ear infection can be caused by wet ears that have not been dried properly after a bath or swimming, ear wax buildup, untreated ear mites, buildup of foreign matter such as seeds or pollen or hair growth inside the ear canal.

First of all, you should be regularly checking your Shih Tzu's ears so that you will be alerted to any problem before it has the opportunity to become serious.

If you have NOT been keeping an eye on your Shih Tzu's ears, the first sign of an infection may be when you notice your dog constantly scratching an ear, shaking their head or holding their head to one side.

Some dogs will whine when they scratch at their ears, and their balance and coordination may be affected.

Immediately make an appointment to take your Shih Tzu to the veterinarian, who will prescribe medicated ear drops that you will have to apply several times each day until the infection is cured.

Congenital Defects

Congenital defects refer to abnormalities of the body that are present when the Shih Tzu puppy is born. These types of defects may involve any part of the puppy's body or any system or organ within the puppy's body.

Some congenital defects can be slight or minor and may naturally resolve themselves as the puppy grows, while others defects can cause or prevent the normal development and function of the puppy, even to the point of causing early death.

While most of these little dogs, when properly screened and bred by caring and conscientious breeders, will not suffer from many problems, the following is an alphabetical listing of hereditary or genetic conditions that a Shih Tzu "may" suffer from:

Epilepsy

Epileptic seizures can be mild, affecting only a part of the dog's body and passing quickly. Other seizures are disruptive and dramatic and can include the dog falling down, twitching and losing consciousness.

Epilepsy is caused by electrical misfiring in a Shih Tzu's brain. The brain's neurons shoot off too many "move" signals, which lead to seizing muscles.

While epilepsy is considered to be hereditary in most cases, it can also be caused by toxins or tumors.

Hip Dysplasia

While hip dysplasia is generally considered a congenital problem affecting larger breeds of canines, it can also be found in small breed dogs, such as the Shih Tzu.

Hip dysplasia causes weakness and lameness to the rear quarters or back legs, which eventually leads to painful arthritis.

The ball of the hip joint is flat rather than round and does not fit properly into the socket and can occur as a result of several factors outside of genetics.

For instance, environmental factors, such as too much calcium in the puppy's diet, obesity, high protein and calorie diets, and a lack of or too much exercise can be contributing factors.

X-rays will determine diagnosis and treatment of mild conditions can consist of administering pain relievers, whereas surgery will be an option for more severe cases.

Hypoglycemia

Hypoglycemia, more commonly referred to as "low blood sugar," can be a problem for young puppies, especially toy breeds, because they sometimes can forget to eat regularly.

Stress can also bring about low blood sugar because dogs under stress also stop eating.

The signs that your puppy may be suffering from low blood sugar may be difficult to notice at first, but they will eventually start breathing harder, stop playing, move about more slowly and appear tired.

Treatment of this condition is easy, however, it is important to act quickly (especially with puppies). While you can purchase a tube of high protein paste, such as Fori-Cal Gel, Nutri-Cal or Nutri-Stat, the simplest home remedy is to feed your puppy some Karo corn syrup, which will quickly raise their blood sugar levels.

After giving your puppy a teaspoon of syrup, you will notice an improvement in approximately 15 minutes time, and you can also put a little syrup into their drinking water.

Of course, the best way to prevent hypoglycemia is to pay attention and make sure that you observe your puppy eating regular meals. Leaving food out for a puppy all day long is no guarantee that they will remember to eat it when they are hungry.

Hypothyroidism

When the thyroid gland malfunctions and no longer produces a thyroid hormone responsible for proper metabolism, the resulting condition is called "hypothyroidism."

This condition usually affects middle-aged dogs (of any breed) and is commonly a result of immune system problems, which can be diagnosed through blood testing.

Your dog may appear tired, and physical symptoms can include hair loss, weight gain, or muscle loss.

Hypothyroidism is not considered a threat to quality of life, because the disease can be effectively treated with drug therapy. However, if left untreated, it can lead to heart problems.

Patellar Luxation

This slipping or floating kneecap condition is a common defect seen in many smaller breeds of dogs weighing less than 22 pounds, such as the Shih Tzu.

It is also possible that the problem can be caused by accidentally falling or jumping from a height.

Usually the condition will present itself between the ages of 4 and 6 months; females are 1.5 times more likely to be affected than males are.

Often you will see a dog with this problem appear to be skipping down the road occasionally lifting one leg as the kneecap slips out of the patellar groove and the leg locks up. In more severe cases, surgery may be the recommended treatment option to correct this condition.

Portosystemic Shunt

This is a life-threatening congenital defect that results in abnormal circulating of the blood, also called "liver shunt," and is a malformation of the portal vein that transports blood to the liver for cleansing.

If not treated, Portosystemic Shunt (PSS) will lead to seizures, blindness, coma and death. In this condition, some of the dog's blood bypasses the liver, which means that this blood is not cleansed of harmful toxins before it returns to poison the heart and other vital organs. PSS results in toxic effects on the brain as well as other body organs.

A Shih Tzu suffering from PSS may display a wide variety of symptoms, including small size, poor appetite, weak muscles, learning difficulty, poor coordination, vomiting, diarrhea and behavioral problems.

Unless PSS can be successfully treated (which is difficult and not always possible), the affected dog will suffer from progressive dementia due to brain damage that will lead to coma and eventual death.

It is possible to test puppies for PSS using a bile acid stimulation test before a puppy is sold by a breeder.

Treatment of PSS begins with stabilization through medical management to improve the dog's health, consisting of feeding a low protein diet combined with oral administration of antibiotics and lactulose.

Medical treatment will decrease the amount of bacteria in the intestines, which will then minimize the production of toxins.

The next step in treatment will be surgery, which involves surgical narrowing or complete tying off of the abnormal shunt vessel, often a very difficult surgery.

The prognosis is good if the dog survives without succumbing to seizure within the first 1-2 days after surgery.

Stenotic Nares

This is an inherited defect usually affecting flat-faced or short-nosed brachycephalic breeds, such as the Shih Tzu.

Stenotic Nares is a narrow, restricted nostril that reduces the amount of air, thereby causing a strain on breathing, which when left untreated can lead to an enlargement of the heart.

The condition can cause snoring, snorting, grunting, sneezing and sniffling with a clear nasal discharge and can be a common occurrence in the Shih Tzu.

Beside the loud breathing noises you can hear, you will notice that the dog cannot play for very long before having to take a break and rest, and their gums are pale. In severe cases, the newborn puppy does not make it past the weaning phase.

Thankfully, many puppies grow out of the problems as they mature, and if they do not, surgery can correct the problem, which involves cutting the cartilage between the two nostrils.

TIP: a non-surgical remedy often recommended is to replace the Shih Tzu's water bowl with a water bottle similar to those used by rabbits and guinea pigs, so that the dog can drink without getting their nose in the water.

Von Willebrand Disease

This bleeding disorder, which can be mild or moderate, results from a reduced production of glycoprotein, a requirement for proper blood clotting.

A dog suffering from this disease may experience bleeding from the nose, gums or urinary system, as well as intestinal bleeding that could also cause diarrhea.

A Shih Tzu that has Von Willebrand disease, when injured, or during surgery, may suffer from prolonged bleeding, therefore, if it is known that your dog suffers from this condition it will be important to ensure they are not placed in situations that could cause injury.

Again, while your Shih Tzu may never suffer from any of the above list of diseases, it is always a good idea to be aware of the types of problems they "could" suffer from.

For instance, every dog is different, and my healthy Shih Tzu has only suffered from the occasional reverse sneezing episode in over eight years.

Chapter 8 - Daily Feeding and Care

Feeding Puppies

For growing puppies, a general feeding rule of thumb is to feed 10% of the puppy's present body weight or between 2% and 3% of their projected adult weight each day.

Keep in mind that higher energy puppies will require extra protein to help them grow and develop into healthy adult dogs, especially during their first two years of life.

There are now many foods on the market that are formulated for all stages of a dog's life (including the puppy stage).

Puppies will need to be fed smaller meals more frequently throughout the day (3 or 4 times) until they are at least one year of age.

NOTE: choose quality sources of meat protein for healthy puppies and dogs, including beef, buffalo, chicken, duck, fish, hare, lamb, ostrich, pork, rabbit, turkey, venison, or any other source of wild meaty protein.

Feeding Adults

An adult dog will generally need to be fed 2 to 3% of their body weight each day. Read the labels and avoid foods that contain a high amount of grains and other fillers. Choose foods that list high quality meat protein as the main ingredient.

TIP: grated parmesan cheese sprinkled on a dinner will help to stop picky eaters from ignoring their food.

Treats

Since the creation of the first dog treat over 150 years ago, the myriad of choices available on every pet store, feed store and grocery store shelf almost outnumbers those looking forward to eating them.

Today's treats are not just for making us guilty humans feel better because we've left our dog home alone for hours, or because it makes us happy to give our fur friends something they really like, today's treats are designed to improve our dog's health.

Some of us humans treat our dogs just because, others use treats for training purposes, others for health, while still others treat for a combination of reasons.

Whatever reason you choose to give treats to your Shih Tzu, keep in mind that if we treat our dogs too often throughout the day, we may create a picky eater who will no longer want to eat their regular meals.

As well, if the treats we are giving are high calorie, we may be putting our dog's health in jeopardy by allowing them to become overweight.

Generally, the treats you feed should not make up more than approximately 10% of their daily food intake.

The Bad and the Ugly

Rawhide goes through an extensive processing with unhealthy chemicals, the result of which is that the rawhide is no longer food and as such, no longer has to comply with food or health regulations. Ingested rawhide can swell to four times its size, which can cause mild to severe gastric blockages that require surgery.

Pigs Ears are extremely high in fat and processed with unhealthy chemicals that can cause stomach upset, vomiting and diarrhea for many dogs.

Hoof Treats include cow, horse, and pig hooves that are processed with preservatives, including insecticides, lead, bleach, arsenic-based products and antibiotics to kill bacteria, and if all bacteria are not killed, your dog could also suffer from Salmonella poisoning. These can also cause chipping or breaking of your dog's teeth, as well as perforation or blockages in your dog's intestines.

Photo Credit: Janine Scott of Honeyshuchon Shih Tzus

The Good

Hard Treats: there are so many choices of hard or crunchy treats available that come in many varieties of shapes, sizes and flavors, that you may have a difficult time choosing. If your Shih Tzu will eat them, hard treats will help to keep their teeth cleaner.

Whatever you choose, read the labels and make sure that the ingredients are high quality and appropriately sized for your Shih Tzu friend.

Soft Treats: are also available in a wide variety of flavors, shapes and sizes for all the different needs of our fur friends and are often used for training purposes as they have a stronger smell.

Often smaller dogs, such as the Shih Tzu, prefer the soft, chewy treats over the hard, crunchy ones.

Dental Treats: or chews are designed with the specific purpose of helping your Shih Tzu to maintain healthy teeth and gums. They usually require intensive chewing and are often shaped with high ridges and bumps to exercise the jaw and massage gums while removing plaque build-up near the gum line.

Freeze-dried and Jerky Treats: offer a tasty morsel most dogs find irresistible, as they are usually made of simple, meaty ingredients, such as liver, poultry and seafood. These treats are usually light weight and easy to carry around, which means they can also be great as training treats or to take with you when you and your dog go on a long walk.

Human Food Treats: often contain additives and ingredients that are toxic or poisonous to our fur friends, so be very careful when sharing human food as treats for your Shih Tzu. Choose simple, fresh foods with minimal or no processing, such as lean meat, poultry or seafood.

Even today, far too many dog food choices continue to have far more to do with being convenient for us humans to serve than they do with being a well-balanced, healthy food choice for a canine.

Sadly, because dogs will eat pretty much anything, we humans have been guilty of feeding pretty much anything to them for a very long time.

Mother Nature's Design

In order to choose the right food for your Shih Tzu, first it's important to understand a little bit about canine physiology and what Mother Nature intended when she created our furry companions. Perhaps most important when choosing an appropriate diet for our dogs is taking a closer look at our dog's teeth, jaws and digestive tract.

While humans are herbivores who derive energy from eating plants, our canine companions are carnivores, which means they derive their energy and nutrient requirements from eating a diet consisting mainly or exclusively of the flesh of animals, birds or fish.

The Canine Teeth and Jaw

The first part of your dog you will want to take a good look at when considering what to feed them will be their teeth.

Unlike humans, who are equipped with wide, flat molars for grinding grains, vegetables and other plant-based materials, canine teeth are all pointed because they are designed to rip, shred and tear into meat and bone.

Another obvious consideration when choosing an appropriate food source for our fur friends is the fact that every canine is born equipped with powerful jaws and neck muscles for the specific purpose of being able to pull down and tear apart their hunted prey.

The structure of the jaw of every canine is such that it opens widely to hold large pieces of meat and bone, while the mechanics of a dog's jaw permits only vertical (up and down) movement that is designed for crushing.

The Canine Digestive Tract

A dog's digestive tract is short and simple and designed to move their natural choice of food (hide, meat and bone) quickly through their systems.

The canine digestive system is simply unable to properly break down vegetable matter, which is why whole vegetables look pretty much the same going into your dog as they do coming out the other end.

Given the choice, most dogs would never choose to eat plants and grains or vegetables and fruits over meat, however, we humans continue to feed them a kibble-based diet that contains high amounts of vegetables, fruits and grains and low amounts of meat.

Part of this is because we've been taught that it's a healthy, balanced diet for humans, and therefore, we believe that it must be the same for our dogs, and part of this is because all the fillers that make up our dog's food are less expensive and easier to process than meat.

How much healthier and long lived might our beloved Shih Tzu be if instead of largely ignoring nature's design for our canine companions, we chose to feed them whole, unprocessed, species-appropriate food with the main ingredient being meat?

Whatever you decide to feed your dog, keep in mind that just as too much wheat, other grains and other fillers in our human diet is having a detrimental effect on our health, the same can be very true for our best fur friends.

Our dogs are also suffering from many of the same life-threatening diseases that are rampant in our human society as a direct result of consuming a diet high in genetically altered, impure, processed and packaged foods.

What Is the Best Food?

The dog food industry is very big business, and because there are now almost limitless choices, there is much confusion and endless debate when it comes to answering the question, "What is the best food for my dog?"

Educating yourself by talking to experts and reading everything you can find on the subject, plus taking into consideration several relevant factors, will help to answer the dog food question.

Photo Credit: Pam Crump of JiDu De ShenTi Shih Tzu

For instance, where you live may dictate what sorts of foods you have access to. Other factors to consider will include the particular requirements of your dog, such as their age, energy and activity levels.

Next will be expense, time and quality. While we all want to give our dogs the best food possible, many humans lead very busy lives and cannot, for instance, prepare their own dog food, but still want to feed a high quality diet that fits within their budget.

The BARF Diet

While some of us believe we are killing ourselves as well as our dogs with processed foods, others believe that there are dangers in feeding raw foods.

Raw feeding advocates believe that the ideal diet for their dog is one that would be very similar to what a dog living in the wild would have access to, and these canine guardians are often opposed to feeding their dog any sort of commercially manufactured pet foods.

On the other hand, those opposed to feeding their dogs a raw or Biologically Appropriate Raw Food (BARF) diet believe that the risks associated with food-borne illnesses during the handling and feeding of raw meats outweigh the purported benefits.

Interestingly, even though the United States Food and Drug Administration (FDA) states that they do not advocate a raw diet for dogs, they do advise that for those who wish to take this route, following basic hygiene guidelines for handling raw meat can minimize any associated risks.

Further, high pressure pasteurization (HPP), which is high pressure, water-based technology for killing bacteria, is

USDA approved for use on organic and natural food products and is being utilized by many commercial raw pet food manufacturers.

Raw meats purchased at your local grocery store contain a much higher level of acceptable bacteria than raw food produced for dogs, because the meat purchased for human consumption is meant to be cooked, which will kill any bacteria that might be present.

This means that canine guardians feeding their dogs a raw food diet can be quite certain that commercially prepared raw foods sold in pet stores will be safer than raw meats purchased in grocery stores.

Many guardians of high energy, working breed dogs will agree that their dogs thrive on a raw or BARF diet and strongly believe that the potential benefits of feeding a raw dog food diet are many, including:

- Healthy, shiny coats
- Decreased shedding
- Fewer allergy problems
- Healthier skin
- Cleaner teeth
- Fresher breath
- Higher energy levels
- Improved digestion
- Smaller stools
- Strengthened immune system
- Increased mobility in arthritic pets
- General increase or improvement in overall health

All dogs, whether working breed or lap dogs, are amazing athletes in their own right, therefore every dog deserves to be fed the best food available.

A raw diet is a direct evolution of what dogs ate before they became our domesticated pets and we turned toward commercially prepared, easy-to-serve dry dog food that required no special storage or preparation.

The Dehydrated Diet

Dehydrated dog food comes in both raw and cooked forms, and these foods are usually air dried to reduce moisture to the level where bacterial growth is inhibited.

The appearance of dehydrated dog food is very similar to dry kibble, and the typical feeding methods include adding warm water before serving, which makes this type of diet both healthy for our dogs and convenient for us to serve.

Dehydrated recipes are made from minimally processed fresh whole foods to create a healthy and nutritionally balanced meal that will meet or exceed the dietary requirements for healthy canines.

Dehydrating removes only the moisture from the fresh ingredients, which usually means that because the food has not already been cooked at a high temperature, more of the overall nutrition is retained.

A dehydrated diet is a convenient way to feed your dog a nutritious diet, because all you have to do is add warm

water and wait five minutes while the food re-hydrates so
your Shih Tzu can enjoy a warm meal.

The Kibble Diet

While many canine guardians are starting to take a closer
look at the food choices they are making for their furry
companions, there is no mistaking that the convenience and
relative economy of dry dog food kibble, which had its
beginnings in the 1940s, continues to be the most popular
pet food choice for most humans.

While feeding a high-quality, bagged kibble diet that has
been flavored to appeal to dogs and supplemented with
vegetables and fruits to appeal to humans may keep most
every Shih Tzu companion happy and healthy, you will
need to decide whether this is the best diet for them.

Exercise

Every dog is an athlete, and therefore they need daily
exercise to say fit and healthy. While the energetic Shih Tzu
is no exception to this rule, often you will see these dogs
packing extra weight, which is purely a result of humans
feeding too much and exercising too little.

Every Shih Tzu will love going for walks with their
guardian several times every day, and this will help to keep
them at a healthy weight.

As well, taking your Shih Tzu for a disciplined walk where
they are on leash and walking beside you without straining

on the leash or trying to lead you will reinforce that you are the boss and they are the follower.

Any type of disciplined exercise you can engage in with your Shih Tzu will help to exercise both their body and their mind and will burn off daily energy reserves so that your pet will be a happy and contented lap dog.

Photo Credit: Pam Crump of JiDu De ShenTi Shih Tzu

If you find that your Shih Tzu is being a pest by chewing inappropriate items around the home or being demanding of your time, this is likely because they are not being exercised often enough or long enough.

Playtime

Every dog needs some regular playtime each day, and the Shih Tzu is no exception to this general care rule, because this is a loving, energetic companion.

Every Shih Tzu will be different with respect to what types of games they may enjoy. For instance, most Shih Tzu will enjoy a game of ball, although generally they are missing the "retriever" gene and may chase after a ball but then not bring it back. Others may enjoy a gentle tug-o-war with a soft rope, or chasing a soft toy, while some Shih Tzu love learning tricks.

Most Shih Tzu will love a fun game of "Search," where you ask your Shih Tzu to "Sit/Stay" while you hide a favorite treat that they then have to sniff out. Of course, the reward in this game is getting to eat the treat.

After a disciplined walk with your Shih Tzu, they will also enjoy being given the opportunity for some off-leash freedom to run, sniff about, play and socialize with other like-sized dogs.

Generally, they will not enjoy playing with large dogs and may display big attitude if a large, lumbering Lab or highly energetic Boxer tries to engage them.

Chapter 9 - Shih Tzu Training

Generally speaking, the Shih Tzu will be easy to train so long as their guardian is gentle and patient, because using harsh or loud training methods will frighten a Shih Tzu and cause them to shut down.

All training sessions should be happy and fun filled, with plenty of rewards and positive reinforcement, which will ensure that your Shih Tzu is an excellent student who looks forward to learning new commands and tricks.

Dog Whispering or Dog Training?

Many people can be confused when they need professional help with their dog, because for eons, if you needed help with your dog, you contacted a "dog trainer" or took your dog to "puppy classes" where your dog would learn how to sit or stay.

The difference between a dog trainer and a dog whisperer would be that a "dog trainer" teaches a dog how to perform certain tasks, and a "dog whisperer" alleviates behavior problems by teaching humans what they need to do to keep their particular dog happy.

Often, depending on how soon the guardian has sought help, this can mean that the dog in question has developed some pretty serious issues, such as aggressive barking, lunging, biting or attacking other dogs, pets or people.

Dog whispering is often an emotional roller coaster ride for the humans involved that unveils many truths when they finally realize that it has been their actions (or inactions) that have likely caused the unbalanced behavior that their dog is now displaying.

Once solutions are provided, the relief for both dog and human can be quite palpable and cathartic when they realize that with the correct direction, they can indeed live a happy life with their dog.

All specific methods of training, such as "clicker training," fall outside of what every dog needs to be happy, because training your dog to respond to a clicker, which you can easily do on your own, and then letting them sleep in your bed, eat from your plate and any other multitude of things humans allow are what makes the dog unbalanced and causes behavior problems.

I always say to people, don't wait until you have a severe problem before getting some dog whispering or professional help of some sort, because "With the proper training, Man can learn to be dog's best friend."

Puppy Training

Puppy training can begin as soon as you bring your Shih Tzu puppy home from the breeder.

Most humans believe that they need to take their puppy to puppy classes, and generally speaking, this is a good idea for any young Shih Tzu (after they have had their vaccinations), because it will help to get them socialized.

Three Most Important Words

"Come," "Sit" and "Stay" will be the three most important words you will ever teach your Shih Tzu puppy.

These three basic commands will ensure that your Shih Tzu remains safe in almost every circumstance.

For instance, when your puppy correctly learns the "Come" command, you can always quickly bring them back to your side should danger be approaching.

When you teach your Shih Tzu puppy the "Sit" and "Stay" commands, you will be further establishing your leadership role. A puppy who understands that their human guardian is their leader will be a safe and happy follower.

Choosing a Discipline Sound

Choosing a "discipline sound" that will be the same for every human family member will make it much easier for your puppy to learn what they can or cannot do.

The best types of sounds are short and sharp. It doesn't really matter what the sound is, so long as everyone in the family agrees to use the same sound. A sound that is very effective for most puppies and dogs is a simple "UH" sound said sharply and with emphasis.

Most puppies and dogs respond immediately to this sound and if caught in the middle of doing something they are not supposed to be doing will quickly stop and give you their attention or back away from what they were doing.

Beginner Leash Lesson

You need a 4- or 6-foot leash and a properly sized Martingale training collar that fits your puppy.

TIP: during early leash lessons, you can also put your Shih Tzu puppy in a harness and clip an extra leash onto the harness, so that you can easily lift them over cigarette butts or other enticing pieces of garbage they may want to put in their mouth.

The most important bonding exercise you will experience with your new Shih Tzu puppy is when you go out for your daily walks together.

Far too many humans get lazy or impatient at this early and very impressionable time in a puppy's life and simply ignore the importance of this critical training time that is not only important for your puppy's exercise, but also establishes you as their leader.

Too many guardians of small puppies simply pick up their puppy and carry them outside to relieve themselves, because they are too impatient to wait for the puppy to understand how the collar and leash work.

Carrying a puppy does not help them learn the routine that will be required of them once they become adults and can also create an unstable relationship between the guardian and the Shih Tzu puppy.

Even though a Shih Tzu is able to self-exercise to some degree when spending a lot of their time indoors, always exercising inside will not help to fulfill their natural roaming urges, because every dog instinctually needs to roam their territory.

When you take your new Shih Tzu puppy outside for walks on leash every day, you will be engaging them in valuable multi-tasking training, including:

• The discipline of following their leader.
• Learning to walk on leash.

• Expanding their knowledge of different smells.
• Exercising both their body and their mind.
• Gently growing and developing bones and muscles.
• Socialization with other humans and animals.
• Experience of different environments.
• Trust and respect of their guardian.

Never underestimate the value of daily walks with your Shih Tzu.

As soon as you bring your new puppy home, you will want to teach them how to walk at your side while on leash without pulling.

Thankfully, when you bring your new puppy home, you will have many opportunities for leash training in combination with potty training, because every time your puppy needs to go out to relieve themselves, you can slip on their Martingale training collar and snap on that leash.

During your first on-leash walk, your Shih Tzu puppy may struggle or fight against having a collar around their neck, because the sensation will be new to them. However, at the same time they will want to go with you, so exercise patience and encourage them to walk with you.

Be careful never to drag them, and if they pull backward and refuse to walk forward with you, simply stop for a moment, while keeping slight forward tension on the leash until your Shih Tzu puppy gives up and moves forward.

Immediately reward them with your happy praise, and if they have a favorite treat, this can be an added incentive when teaching them to walk on their leash.

Always walk your puppy on your left side with the leash slack so that they learn that walking with you is a relaxing experience. Keep the leash short enough so that they do not have enough slack to get in front of you.

If they begin to create tension in the leash by pulling forward or to the side, simply stop moving, get them back beside you and start over.

Be patient and consistent with your puppy and very soon they will understand exactly where their walking position is and will walk easily beside you without any pulling or leash tension.

Remember that walking with a new puppy is an exciting experience for them, as they will want to sniff everything and explore their new world, so give them lots of understanding and don't expect them to be perfect.

Extendable NO - NO

If you've been thinking about getting one of those extendable leashes that seem to be so popular, do your Shih Tzu and yourself a great big favor and don't.

The extendable leash can create far more problems for the humans than you might imagine.

A few basic reasons for not joining the ranks of the extendable leash craze are because these types of leashes:

- Allow the dog to be in the leader position.
- Make the guardian the follower.
- Are tripping hazards.
- Offer little or no control to the handler.
- Are clumsy and difficult to hold onto.
- Create lazy guardians who are not paying attention.

The Stubborn Adolescent

The adolescent period in a young Shih Tzu's life, between the ages of 6 and 12 months, is the transitional stage of both physical and psychological development when they are physically almost full grown in size, yet their minds are still developing, and they are testing their boundaries and the limits that their human companions will endure.

This can be a dangerous time in a puppy's life, because this is when they start to make decisions on their own, which can lead to developing unwanted behaviors.

Learning how to make decisions on their own would be perfectly normal and desirable if your Shih Tzu puppy was living in the wild, amongst a pack of dogs, because it would be necessary for their survival.

However, when living within a human environment, your puppy must always adhere to human rules, and it will be up to their human guardians to continue their vigilant, watchful guidance in order to make sure that they do.

Many humans are lulled into a false sense of security when their new Shih Tzu puppy reaches the age of approximately six months, because the puppy has been well socialized and long since been house trained.

The real truth is that the serious work is only now beginning, and the humans and their new Shih Tzu puppy could be in for a time of testing that could seriously challenge the relationship and leave the humans wondering if they made the right decision. The trust and respect that has been previously built can be damaged, sometimes irreparably.

Photo Credit: Victoria Grugan of Jardhu Shih Tzu

While not all puppies will experience a noticeable adolescent period of craziness, most young dogs do commonly exhibit at least some of the usual adolescent behaviors, including reverting to previous puppy behaviors.

Some of these adolescent behaviors might include destructive chewing of objects they have previously shown no interest in, selective hearing or ignoring previously learned commands, displaying aggressive behavior, jumping on everyone, barking at everything that moves, or even reverting to relieving themselves in the house, even though they were house trained months ago.

Keeping your cool and recognizing these adolescent signs are the first step toward helping to make this transition period easier on your puppy and all family members.

The first step to take that can help keep raging hormones at bay is to spay or neuter your Shih Tzu puppy just prior to the onset of adolescence, at around five or six months of age. While spaying or neutering a Shih Tzu puppy will not eliminate the adolescent phase, it will certainly help.

Once your Shih Tzu puppy has been spayed or neutered, you will want to become more active with your young dog, both mentally and physically, by providing them with continued and more complex, disciplined exercises.

This can be accomplished by enrolling your adolescent Shih Tzu in a dog whispering session to make sure that necessary rules and boundaries are in place, or a more advanced obedience class that will help them to continue their socialization skills while also developing their brain.

When your Shih Tzu is provided with sufficient daily exercise and continued socialization that provides interest and expands their mind, they will be able to transition through the adolescent stage of their life much more seamlessly.

Yelling Makes it Worse

If your Shih Tzu puppy happens to be especially unruly during their adolescent phase, you will need to simply limit their opportunities for making mistakes.

It does absolutely no good to yell at your Shih Tzu puppy for engaging in behavior you are not happy with, and in fact, yelling will only desensitize your young dog from listening to any of your commands.

Further, although you may eventually get the results you want, if you yell loud enough, your puppy will then be reacting out of fear, rather than respect, and this is not the type of relationship you want to have.

Displaying calm, yet assertive energy is the ONLY energy that will help your adolescent puppy understand what is required of them.

All other human emotions are "read" by puppies and dogs as being unstable, and not only will they not understand you, they will not respect you for displaying these types of confusing energies.

Make sure that your Shih Tzu is within eyesight at all times, so that if they do find an opportunity to make a mistake, you can quickly show them what is permitted and what is not.

Keeping on top of house training is also a good idea during the adolescent period of your puppy's life, because some adolescent puppies may forget that they are already house trained.

This means actually taking the time to be involved in the process by leashing up your Shih Tzu and physically taking them outside whenever they need to relieve themselves.

This sort of a routine is also a disciplined exercise that will help to reinforce in your puppy's mind that you are the boss.

Rewarding Unwanted Behavior

It is very important to recognize that any attention paid to an out-of-control, adolescent puppy, even negative attention, is likely going to be exciting and rewarding for your Shih Tzu puppy.

Chasing after a puppy when they have taken something they are not supposed to have, picking them up when they are barking or showing aggression, pushing them off when they jump on you or other people, or yelling when they refuse to come when called, are all forms of attention that can actually be rewarding for most puppies.

It will be your responsibility to provide structure for your puppy, which will include finding acceptable and safe ways to allow your puppy to vent their energy without being destructive or harmful to others.

Basic First Commands

All that's necessary for effectively teaching or reinforcing your puppy's basic first commands is a calm, consistent approach, combined with endless patience.

Most puppies are ready to begin simple training at about 10 to 12 weeks of age, however, be careful not to overdo it when they are under six months of age, as their attention span will be short and they will tire easily.

Make training sessions positive and fun and no more than 5 or 10 minutes, with lots of praise and/or treats so that your puppy will be eagerly looking forward to their next session.

Also, introduce the hand signals that go along with the verbal commands so that once they learn both, you can remove the verbal commands and only use hand signals.

Basic Hand Signals

Hand signal training is by far the most useful and efficient training method for every dog, including the Shih Tzu.

This is because all too often we inundate our canine companions with a great deal of chatter and noise that they really do not understand, because English is not their first language.

Contrary to what some humans might think, the first language of a Shih Tzu, or any dog, is a combination of sensing energy and watching body language, which requires no spoken word or sound.

Therefore, when we humans take the time to teach our dog hand signals for all their basic commands, we are communicating with them at a level they instinctively understand, plus we are helping them to become focused and attentive followers, as they must watch us to understand what is required of them.

Come

While most puppies are capable of learning commands and tricks at a surprisingly young age, the first and most important command you need to teach your puppy is the recall or "Come" command.

The hand signal for "Come" is your arms spread wide open. This is a command they can see from a great distance. Always show the hand signal for the command at the same time you say the word.

Begin the "Come" command inside your home. Go into a larger room, such as your living room area. Place your puppy in front of you and attach their leash or a longer line to their collar while you back away from them a few feet.

Say the command "Come" in an excited voice and hold your arms open wide. If they do not immediately come to you, gently give a tug on the leash so that they understand that they are supposed to move toward you. When they come to you praise them and give a treat they really enjoy.

Once your puppy can accomplish a "Come" command almost every time inside your home, you can then graduate them to a nearby park or quiet outside area where you will repeat the process.

You may want to purchase an extra long line (25 or 50 feet) so that you are always attached to your Shih Tzu puppy and can encourage them in the right direction should they become distracted.

At your leisure, firmly ask them to "Come" and show the hand signal. If they do not immediately come to you, give a firm tug with the lunge line so that they understand what you are asking of them.

If they still do not "Come" toward you, simply reel them in until they are in front of you, praise them and give a treat. Then let them wander about again, until you are ready to ask them to "Come."

Sit

The "Sit" and "Stay" commands are both easy commands to teach, and in combination with the "Come" command, will help to keep your Shih Tzu puppy safe and out of danger in most every circumstance. Find a quiet time to teach these commands when your puppy is not tired.

Every time you take your Shih Tzu out for a walk, get into the habit of asking them to sit while you put on their leash — then ask them to sit again and calmly wait while you put on your shoes.

Most dogs will sit when you ask them while you put on their leash, and as soon as the leash is on, and you are busy putting on your coat or shoes, they get excited and stand up; ask them to sit again and calmly wait while you are getting yourself ready.

Ask your puppy to "Sit," and if they do not yet understand the command, hold a treat over their head, which can cause them to automatically sit, or show them what you mean by gently squeezing with your thumb and middle finger the area across the back that joins with their back legs.

Do not just push or force them down into a sit, as this can cause damage to their back or joints. When they sit, give them a treat and praise them.

When you say the word "Sit," at the same time show them the hand signal for this command, which is bending your arm at the elbow and raising your right hand, palm open facing upward, toward your shoulder.

Slowly remove the treats as reward and replace the treat with a "life reward," such as a chest rub or a thumbs up signal and your happy smile.

Stay

Once your Shih Tzu puppy can reliably "Sit," say the word "Stay" and hold your outstretched arm palm open toward their head and back away a few steps.

If they try to follow, calmly say "No" and put them back into "Sit." Give a treat and then say again, "Stay," with the hand signal and back away a few steps. Continue to practice this until your dog understands that you want them to stay sitting and not move toward you.

With all commands, when your Shih Tzu is just learning, be patient and always reward them with a treat and your happy praise for a job well done.

TIP: use your dominant hand for the "Stay" command and you will have better results because the strongest energy emanates from the palm of your dominant hand. For instance, if you are right handed, use your right hand.

Once your puppy is sitting and staying, you can then ask them to "Come." Don't forget to use the open arms hand signal for "Come."

I would encourage you to be extra excited when training the "Come" command, so that your puppy will always enjoy correctly responding and immediately come running to you because they know they will receive either a tasty treat, your happy praise or both.

Otherwise, the only time you will show some excitement is when you are praising a command well executed.

You do not want your puppy to get the idea that humans are a source of excitement, because this can lead to many other problems in later life.

Practice these three basic commands everywhere you go, and pretty soon you will have an automatically sitting puppy who impresses all your neighbors, because they sit whenever you stop moving without you saying the command or giving the signal.

First Tricks

When teaching your Shih Tzu their first tricks, in order to give them extra incentive, find a small treat that they would do anything to get, and give the treat as rewards and to help solidify a good performance.

Most dogs will be extra attentive during training sessions when they know that they will be rewarded with their favorite treats.

If your Shih Tzu is less than six months old when you begin teaching them tricks, keep your training sessions short (no more than 5 or 10 minutes) and make them lots of fun.

As your Shih Tzu becomes an adult, you can extend your sessions because they will be able to maintain their focus for longer periods of time.

Shake a Paw

Who doesn't love a dog who knows how to shake a paw? This is one of the easiest tricks to teach your Shih Tzu.

TIP: most dogs are naturally either right or left pawed. If you know which paw your dog favors, ask them to shake this paw.

Find a quiet place to practice, without noisy distractions or other pets, and stand or sit in front of your dog. Place them in the sitting position and hold a treat in your left hand.

Say the command "Shake" while putting your right hand behind their left or right paw and pulling the paw gently toward yourself until you are holding their paw in your hand. Immediately praise them and give them the treat.

Most dogs will learn the "Shake" trick very quickly, and in no time at all, once you put out your hand, your Shih Tzu will immediately lift their paw and put it into your hand, without your assistance or any verbal cue.

Practice every day until they are 100% reliable with this trick, and then it will be time to add another trick to their repertoire

Roll Over

You will find that just like your Shih Tzu is naturally either right or left pawed, that they will also naturally want to roll either to the right or the left side. Take advantage of this by asking your dog to roll to the side they naturally prefer.

Sit with your dog on the floor and put them in a lie down position. Hold a treat in your hand and place it close to their nose without allowing them to grab it, and while they are in the lying position, move the treat to the right or left side of their head so that they have to roll over to get to it.

You will very quickly see which side they want to naturally roll to, and once you see this, move the treat to that side. Once they roll over to that side, immediately give them the treat and praise them.

You can say the verbal cue "Over" while you demonstrate the hand signal motion (moving your right hand in a half circular motion) from one side of their head to the other.

Sit Pretty

While this trick is a little more complicated, and most dogs pick up on it very quickly, remember that this trick requires balance, and every dog is different, so always exercise patience.

Find a quiet space with few distractions and sit or stand in front of your dog and ask them to "Sit."

Have a treat nearby (on a countertop or table) and when they sit, use both of your hands to lift up their front paws into the sitting pretty position, while saying the command

"Sit Pretty." Help them balance in this position while you praise them and give them the treat.

Once your Shih Tzu can do the balancing part of the trick quite easily without your help, sit or stand in front of your dog while asking them to "Sit Pretty" and hold the treat above their head, at the level their nose would be when they sit pretty.

If they attempt to stand on their back legs to get the treat, you may be holding the treat too high, which will encourage them to stand up on their back legs to reach it. Go back to the first step and put them back into the "Sit" position and again lift their paws while their backside remains on the floor.

The hand signal for "Sit Pretty" is a straight arm held over your dog's head with a closed fist.

Make this a fun and entertaining time for your Shih Tzu and practice a few times every day until they can "Sit Pretty" on hand signal command every time you ask.

TIP: place your Shih Tzu beside a wall when first teaching this trick so that they can use the wall to help their balance.

A young Shih Tzu puppy should be able to easily learn these basic tricks before they are six months old, and when you are patient and make your training sessions short and fun for your dog, they will be eager to learn more.

Adult Activities

When your Shih Tzu is a full grown adult (approximately two years of age), now is the time that you can begin more complicated or advanced training sessions. They will enjoy it and when you have the desire and patience, there is no end to the tricks you can teach a willing Shih Tzu.

Rally Obedience

Rally Obedience (RallyO) is a fun canine sport that is less strict than regular Obedience, in which the dog and guardian (handler) complete a course that has been designed by the rally judge.

The judge signals the handler (or guardian) to begin, and then both dog and guardian begin navigation of the course, at their own pace, which could include anywhere from 10 to 20 stations that require them to perform different tasks.

For instance, a beginner's course may include heel, sits, turns, pace changes, sit-stay or elements of recall (come). As the dog gains skill, more difficult elements are added into the courses that help to improve you and your dog's performance levels and confidence.

The purpose of RallyO is to promote positive relationships between dogs and owners based on trust and respect.

Everyone can participate, whether purebred show dogs, mixed breeds, handicapped guardians or 3-legged dogs, because the whole idea is for everyone to have fun together, and every dog and guardian has something special to offer.

Currently, the CKC is the only organization that restricts competition to purebred dogs.

Agility

Agility is a fun and fast dog sport in which the dog's guardian or handler directs their off-leash dog through an obstacle course without food or toys as incentives and without touching either the dog or the obstacles in the course.

Control of the dog is limited to voice, movement and various body signals, which means that in order for your Shih Tzu to be able to successfully compete, they must already know basic commands, such as sit, come, stay, up and down while they are closely focused on you.

Musical Canine Freestyle

This freestyle, modern dog sport put to music is known by several names, including "musical canine freestyle," "freestyle dance" and "canine freestyle."

This sport, which mixes music with dance and obedience training to allow for fun, entertaining and creative communication between dogs and their handlers or guardians, has become so popular that dogs and humans can now compete in many countries worldwide.

Chapter 10 - Poisonous Foods & Plants

Harmful Foods

While some dogs are smart enough not to want to eat foods that can harm or kill them, other canine companions will eat absolutely anything they can get their teeth on.

As conscientious guardians for our fur friends, it will always be our responsibility to make certain that when we share our homes with a dog, we never leave foods that could be toxic or lethal to them easily within their reach.

While there are many foods that can be toxic to a Shih Tzu, the following alphabetical list contains some of the more common foods that can seriously harm or even kill our dogs including:

Bread Dough: if your dog eats bread dough, their body heat will cause the dough to rise inside the stomach and alcohol is produced. Shih Tzu that have eaten bread dough may experience stomach bloating, abdominal pain, vomiting, disorientation and depression.

Broccoli: while it may cause stomach upset, it probably won't be very harmful unless the amount eaten is more than 10% of the dog's total daily diet.

Chocolate: contains a chemical that is toxic to dogs in large enough quantities. It is also contains caffeine, which is found in coffee, tea and certain soft drinks.

Caffeine: beverages containing caffeine (like soda, tea, coffee, chocolate) act as stimulants and can accelerate your dog's heartbeat to a dangerous level. Dogs eating caffeine-containing products have been known to have seizures, some of which are fatal.

Cooked Bones: can be extremely hazardous for a dog because cooking makes the bone brittle, which in turn can cause the bone to more easily break apart or splinter when the dog chews on them.

Pieces of bone that have splintered are often sharp and could become lodged between teeth or stuck in a dog's throat, causing choking, and if they swallow splinters, these could puncture the intestines or stomach lining.

Especially dangerous are cooked chicken and turkey legs, pork chops, veal bones or ham bones.

Grapes and Raisins: can cause acute (sudden) kidney failure in dogs. While it is unknown what the toxic agent is in this fruit, clinical signs can occur within 24 hours of eating and include vomiting, diarrhea and lethargy.

Garlic and Onions: contain chemicals that damage red blood cells by rupturing them so that they lose their ability to carry oxygen effectively, which leaves the dog short of oxygen, causing what is called "hemolytic anemia."

NOTE: fresh, cooked and/or powdered garlic or onions are commonly found in baby food, which is sometimes given to dogs when they are sick, therefore, be certain to carefully read food labels before feeding to your Shih Tzu.

Macadamia Nuts: are commonly found in candies and chocolates. The clinical signs in dogs having eaten these nuts include depression, weakness, vomiting, tremors, joint pain and pale gums.

Mushrooms: mushroom poisoning can be fatal if certain species of mushrooms are eaten. The most commonly reported severely toxic species of mushroom in the U.S. is Amanita phalloides (Death Cap mushroom), which is also quite a common species found in most parts of Britain and Canada. Other Amanita species are also toxic.

Eating them can cause severe liver disease and neurological disorders. If you suspect your dog has eaten these mushrooms, immediately take them to your veterinarian, as the recommended treatment is to induce vomiting and to give activated charcoal.

Pits and Seeds: many seeds and pits found in a variety of fruits, including apples, apricots, cherries, pears and plums, contain cyanogenic glycosides that can cause cyanide poisoning in your Shih Tzu.

The symptoms of cyanide poisoning usually occur within 15-20 minutes to a few hours after eating and can include initial excitement, followed by rapid respiration rate, salivation, voiding of urine and feces, vomiting, muscle spasm, staggering and coma before death.

Photo Credit: Susan Kilgore of Fantasy Shih Tzu

Raw Salmon or Trout: Salmon Poisoning Disease (SPD) can cause a problem for dogs who are fed uncooked salmon or trout, because they could then be exposed to SPD when they eat a fish that is already infected.

Fish eat snails and some species of snails are infected with a difficult-to-pronounce bacteria called "nanophyteus salmincola," therefore, when the fish eats an infected snail, and then the dog eats the fish, within 5-7 days the dog will show symptoms similar to canine parvovirus, which when left untreated has a 90% chance of killing the dog.

Preventing this problem is simple – cook all fish before feeding it to your Shih Tzu, and if you are worried that your dog may have eaten raw salmon or trout, immediately seek veterinary assistance.

Tobacco: all forms of tobacco can be deadly to your dog. This includes chewing tobacco, gum or patches. Signs that your dog has been poisoned by tobacco can rapidly appear, such as drooling, panting, vomiting, diarrhea, accelerated heart rate, twitching, collapse and coma, which will lead to cardiac arrest and death.

Tomatoes: contain atropine, which can cause dilated pupils, tremors and irregular heartbeat.

Xylitol: is an artificial sweetener found in products such as gum, candy, mints, toothpaste and mouthwash that is recognized by the National Animal Poison Control Center to be a risk to dogs.

Please be aware that the above list is just some of the more common foods that can be toxic or fatal.

Poisonous Household Plants

Many common house plants are actually poisonous to our canine companions, and although many dogs simply will ignore house plants, some will attempt to eat anything, especially puppies who want to taste everything in their new world.

More than 700 plant species contain toxins that may harm or be fatal to puppies or dogs depending on the size of the puppy or dog and how much they may eat.

Poison Proof Your Home

You can learn about many potentially toxic and poisonous sources both inside and outside your home by visiting the ASPCA Animal Poison Control Center website:

http://www.aspca.org/

Always keep your veterinarian's emergency number in a place where you can quickly access it in case you suspect that your dog may have been poisoned.

Knowing what to do if you suspect your dog may have been poisoned and being able to quickly contact the right people could save your Shih Tzu's life.

Outdoor Garden Plants

Many outdoor plants can be toxic or poisonous to your Shih Tzu, therefore, always check what plants are growing in your garden, and if any might be harmful, remove them or make certain that your Shih Tzu puppy or adult dog cannot eat them.

Cornell University's Department of Animal Science lists many different categories of poisonous plants affecting dogs, including house plants, flowering garden plants, vegetable garden plants, plants found in swamps or moist areas, plants found in fields, trees and shrubs, plants found in wooded areas and ornamental plants.

http://www.ansci.cornell.edu/plants/dogs/

Why Do Dogs Eat Grass?

Also, be aware that many puppies and adult dogs will eat grass, just because. They may be bored, or need a little fiber in their diet or just like the taste.

Remember that canines have been natural scavengers for hundreds of years and are always on the lookout for something they can eat.

So long as the grass is healthy and has not been sprayed with toxic chemicals, a little salad, in the form of grass, is a natural part of most every dog's diet, and should only be a concern if you no longer have to mow your lawn.

Chapter 11 - Caring for Aging Dogs

What to Be Aware Of

As a result of advances in veterinary care, improvements in diet and nutrition, and general knowledge concerning proper care of our canine companions, our dogs are able to enjoy longer, healthier lives, and as such, when caring for them we need to be aware of behavioral and physical changes that will affect our dogs as they approach old age.

Depending upon their usual level of health and activity, a Shih Tzu may be entering the senior stage of their life at around 8 to 10 years of age.

Physiological Changes

As our beloved canine companions become senior dogs, they will be suffering from physical aging problems similar to those that affect humans, such as heightened sensitivity to cold and hot weather, pain, stiffness and arthritis, diminished or complete loss of hearing and sight, and inability to control their bowels and bladder. Any of these problems will reduce a dog's willingness to want to exercise.

Behavioral Changes

Further, a senior Shih Tzu may experience behavioral changes resulting from loss of hearing and sight, such as disorientation, fear or startle reactions and overall grumpiness from any number of physical problems that could be causing them pain whenever they move.

Just as research and science has improved our human quality of life in our senior years, the same is becoming true for our canine counterparts, who are able to benefit from dietary supplements and pharmaceutical products to help them be as comfortable as possible in their advancing years.

Of course there will be some inconveniences associated with keeping a dog with advancing years around the home, however, your Shih Tzu deserves no less than to spend their final days in your loving care after they have unconditionally given you their entire lives.

Geriatric Dogs

Being aware of the changes that are likely occurring in a senior dog will help you to better care for them during their geriatric years.

For instance, most dogs will experience hearing loss and visual impairment, and depending upon which goes first (hearing or sight) you will need to alter how you communicate. For instance, if a dog's hearing is compromised, then using more hand signals will be helpful.

Deaf dogs will still be able to hear louder noises and feel vibrations, therefore hand clapping, knocking on furniture or walls, using a loud clicker or stomping your foot on the floor may be a way to get their attention.

If a senior dog loses their eyesight, most dogs will still be able to easily navigate their familiar surroundings, and you will only need to be extra watchful on their behalf when taking them to unfamiliar territory.

If they still have their hearing, you will be able to assist your dog with verbal cues and commands. Dogs that have lost both their hearing and their sight will need to be close to you so that they can relax and not feel nervous, and so that you can communicate by touching parts of their body.

Generally speaking, even when a dog becomes blind and/or deaf, their powerful sense of smell is still functioning, which means that they will be able to smell where you are and navigate their environment by using their nose.

More Frequent Bathroom Breaks

Bathroom breaks may need to become more frequent in older dogs that may lose their ability to hold it for longer periods of time, so be prepared to be more watchful and to offer them opportunities to go outside more frequently during the day.

You may also want to place a pee pad near the door in case they just can't hold it long enough, or if you have not already taught them to bathroom on an indoor potty patch, or pee pad, now may be the time for this alternative bathroom arrangement.

A dog who has been house trained for years will feel the shame and upset of not being able to hold it long enough to get to their regular bathroom location, so be kind and do whatever you need to do to help them not to have to feel bad about failing bowel or bladder control.

Cognitive Decline

Our pets may also begin to show signs of cognitive decline or disorientation and changes in the way their brain functions, similar to what happens to humans suffering from Alzheimer's, where they start to wander about aimlessly, sometimes during the middle of the night.

Make sure that if this is happening with your Shih Tzu at nighttime, that they cannot accidentally harm themselves by falling down stairs or getting into areas where they could injure themselves.

Make a Senior Dog Comfortable

Regular Checkups

During this time in your Shih Tzu's life, when their immune systems become weakened and they may be experiencing pain, you will want to get into the habit of taking your senior Shih Tzu for regular vet checkups.

Photo Credit: Victoria Grugan of Jardhu Shih Tzu

Take them for a checkup every six months so that early detection of any problems can quickly be attended to and solutions for helping to keep them comfortable can be provided.

No Rough Play

An older Shih Tzu will not have the same energy or willingness to play that they did when they were younger, therefore, do not allow younger children to rough house with an older dog.

Explain to children that they must learn to be gentle and to leave the dog alone when it may want to rest or sleep.

Mild Exercise

Dogs still love going for walks, even when they are getting older and may be slowing down.

Even though an older Shih Tzu will generally have less energy, they still need to exercise, and taking them out regularly for shorter walks will not only make them happy, keeping them moving will help them to live longer and healthier golden years.

Best Quality Food

Everyone has heard the saying "you are what you eat," and for a senior dog, what they eat is even more important, as their digestive system may no longer be functioning at peak performance.

Feeding a high quality, protein-based food will be important for your senior Shih Tzu's continued health.

NOTE: if your older Shih Tzu is overweight, you will want to help them shed excess pounds that will be placing undue stress on their joints and heart. Feed smaller quantities of a higher quality food to help them lose the excess weight.

Clean and Bug Free

The last thing an aging Shih Tzu should have to deal with is the misery of itching and scratching, so make sure that you continue to give them regular baths with the appropriate shampoos and conditioners to keep their coat and skin comfortable and free from dirt or invading parasites.

Plenty of Water

Hydration is essential for helping to keep an older Shih Tzu comfortable.

Water is life-giving for every creature, so make certain that your aging dog has easy access to plenty of clean, fresh water that will help to improve their energy and digestion and also prevent dehydration, which can add to joint stiffness.

Keeping Warm

Just as older humans feel the cold more, so do older dogs. Keeping your senior Shih Tzu warm will help to alleviate some of the pain of their joint stiffness or arthritis.

If there is a draft in the home, generally it will be at floor level, therefore, a bed (ideally heated) that is raised up off of the floor will be warmer for your senior Shih Tzu.

While many dogs seem to be happy with sleeping on the floor, providing them with a padded, soft bed will greatly help to relieve sore spots and joint pain in older dogs.

Your aging Shih Tzu will be more sensitive to extremes in temperature, therefore, make sure that they are comfortable at all times, which means not too hot and not too cold.

Indoor Clothing

Just like humans, aging dogs have more difficulty maintaining a comfortable body temperature.

Therefore, while you most likely already have a selection of outdoor clothing appropriate to the various climate conditions in which you live, you may not have considered keeping your Shih Tzu warm while inside the home.

Now would be the time to consider doggy t-shirts or sweater clothing options to help keep your aging companion comfortably warm both inside and out.

Steps or Stairs

If your Shih Tzu is allowed to sleep on the human couch or chair, but they are having difficulties getting up there as their joints are becoming stiff and painful, consider buying or making them a set of soft foam stairs so that they can easily get up to their favorite snoozing spot.

More Love and Attention

Last, but not least, make sure that you give your senior Shih Tzu lots of love and attention and never leave them alone for long periods of time.

When they are not feeling their best, they will want to be with you all that much more, because you are their guardian whom they trust and love beyond life itself.

What is Euthanasia?

Every veterinarian will have received special training to help provide all incurably ill, injured or aging pets that have come to the end of their natural lives with a humane and gentle death through a process called "euthanasia."

When the time comes, euthanasia, or putting a dog "to sleep," will usually be a two-step process.

First, the veterinarian will inject the dog with a sedative to make them sleepy, calm and comfortable.

Second, the veterinarian will inject a special drug that will peacefully stop their heart.

These drugs work in such a way that the dog will not experience any awareness whatsoever that their life is ending. What they will experience is very similar to falling asleep, or what we humans experience when going under anesthesia during a surgical procedure.

Once the second stage drug has been injected, the entire process takes about 10 to 20 seconds, at which time the veterinarian will then check to make certain that the dog's heart has stopped.

There is no suffering with this process, which is a very gentle and humane way to end a dog's suffering and allow them to peacefully pass on.

When to Help a Dog Transition

The impending loss of a beloved dog is one of the most painfully difficult and emotionally devastating experiences a canine guardian will ever have to face.

For the sake of our faithful companions, because we do not want to prolong their suffering, we humans will have to do our best to assess our dog's situation practically, rather than emotionally, so that we can make the most humane decision for them.

They may be suffering from extreme old age and the inability to even walk to a pee pad or get to the outside to relieve themselves, and thus may be suffering the indignity and shame of regularly soiling their sleeping area. They may have been diagnosed with an incurable illness that is causing them much pain, or they may have been seriously injured.

Whatever the reason for a beloved canine companion's suffering, it will be up to their human guardian to calmly guide their end-of-life experience so that any further discomfort and distress can be minimized.

During this time of uncertainty, you will want to discuss with your veterinarian what signs of suffering may be associated with the dog's particular disease or condition, so that you know what to look for.

Often a dog may still continue to eat or drink despite being distraught, having difficulty breathing, excessively panting, being disoriented or in much pain, and as their caring guardians, we will have to weigh their love of eating against how much they are really suffering in all other areas of their life.

We humans are often tempted to delay the inevitable moment of euthanasia, because we love our dogs so much and cannot bear the thought of the intense grief we know will overwhelm us when we must say our final goodbyes to our beloved companion.

Unfortunately, we may regret that we allowed our dog to suffer too long, and find ourselves wishing that we humans had the option to peacefully let go when we reach such a stage in our own lives.

Grieving a Lost Pet

Some humans have difficulty fully recognizing the terrible grief involved in losing a beloved canine friend.

There will be many who do not understand the close bond we humans can have with our dogs, which is often unlike any we have with our human counterparts.

Your friends may give you pitying looks and try to cheer you up, but if they have never experienced the loss of such a special connection themselves, they may also secretly think you are making too much fuss over "just a dog."

For some of us humans, the loss of a beloved dog is so painful that we decide never to share our lives with another, because the thought of going through the pain of such a loss is unbearable.

Expect to feel terribly sad, tearful and yes, depressed, because those who are close to their canine companions will feel their loss no less acutely than the loss of a human friend or life partner.

The grieving process can take some time to recover from, and some of us never totally recover.

After the loss of a family dog, first you need to take care of yourself by making certain that you remember to eat regular meals and get enough sleep, even though you will feel an almost eerie sense of loneliness.

Losing a beloved dog is a shock to the system that can also affect your concentration and your ability to find joy or be interested in participating in other activities that are a normal part of your daily life.

Other Pets Grieve, Too

Other dogs, cats and pets in the home will also be grieving the loss of a companion, and may display this by acting depressed, being off their food or showing little interest in play or games.

Therefore, you need to help guide your other pets through this grieving process by keeping them busy and interested, taking them for extra walks and finding ways to spend more time with them.

Wait Long Enough

Many people do not wait long enough before attempting to replace a lost pet and will immediately go to the local shelter and rescue a deserving dog. While this may help to distract you from your grieving process, this is not really fair to the new fur member of your family.

Bringing a new pet into a home that is depressed and grieving the loss of a long-time canine member may create behavioral problems for the new dog that will be faced with learning all about their new home while also dealing with the unstable energy of the grieving family.

A better scenario would be to allow yourself the time to properly grieve by waiting a minimum of one month to allow yourself and your family to feel happier and more stable before deciding upon sharing your home with another dog.

Memorials

There are many unique ways to honor the passing of a beloved Shih Tzu, because every one of our fur friends is unique and special to us.

If you have children, you will want to involve them in the process of honoring and remembering their lost friend too.

For instance, you may wish to have your fur friend cremated and preserve their ashes in a special urn or sprinkle their ashes along their favorite walk or along a shoreline where they loved to play.

Perhaps you will want to have a special marker, photo bereavement, photo-engraved Rainbow Bridge Poem or wooden plaque created in honor of your lost friend.

Or, you may wish to keep their memory even closer to you at all times by having a DNA remembrance pendant or bracelet designed.

As well, there are support groups, such as Rainbow Bridge, which is a grief support community, to help you and your family through this painful period of loss and grief.

http://www.rainbowbridge.com

Chapter 12 - Bonus Interview with Susan Kilgore

I hope you have enjoyed reading this guide on Shih Tzu dogs, and we are not quite finished yet. This extra section is an interview which I did with Susan Kilgore, an expert breeder and major dog show winner.

Susan thanks for doing this interview, can you tell us who you are and where you are based?

My name is Susan Kilgore of Green Lake, Wisconsin and I show and breed Shih Tzu using the kennel prefix Fantasy Shih Tzu. I've been enjoying and loving the breed since my first introduction to them in 1985 when a darling black and white male became a part of my family.

I wanted to interview you because it seems to me you have an interesting personal story to tell given your success showing your Shih Tzu dogs.

Perhaps we could start by you telling us what achievements you have just accomplished?

My most current achievements for 2014 include having bred two AKC conformation champions thus far, and I am working on a third, which is a pretty red and white bitch from one of my breedings.

Another achievement this year is an American Shih Tzu Club (ASTC) Register of Merit Award (ROM) for one of my top producing bitches, Fantasy's Hot Line Lynette, who produced 5 AKC champions to date. 4 champions produced by a dam is the ASTC requirement for award qualification, 6 champions for sires.

I've had the pleasure of breeding many titled Shih Tzu in my tenure to include performance and conformation title winners right up to many Best in Show Shih Tzu. My fondest memory and greatest achievement in the breed was undoubtedly to have had a breed win at the Westminster Kennel Club show one year with a close second being owner-handling two Best in Specialty Show winners for these awards.

I've owned over 50 conformation champions of which 36 are AKC champions that I've bred, in addition to many ASTC Register of Merit award winners. One well-known male I purchased and showed became the top champion producing sire in 1994 for the breed and another I bred became, and still holds the fifth All-Time Champion Producer for the breed in history according to the American Kennel Club and American Shih Tzu Club records.

It is heartwarming to know that many of the Shih Tzu I've bred have been loved and appreciated as pet companions and valued producers.

I'm sure a lot of readers think there's lots of mystery behind these dog shows, but how did it start for you and when?

It started in 1985/86 when I found an ad in the Milwaukee Journal Sentinel newspaper for the Greater Milwaukee Shih Tzu Club's fun match to be held in a shopping center called Brookfield Square. I had acquired my first Shih Tzu puppy, Sammy, and fell in love with him, so naturally I was not only interested in attending but in showing him and meeting others in the breed.

It was exciting for me to have this first experience. That's where I saw lovely show quality puppies and adults, met very nice fanciers and immediately applied for club membership. The club name has changed since that time to the Shih Tzu Club of Southeastern Wisconsin. It now offers two AKC licensed specialty shows each year.

I know a lot of readers of this book are just interested in owning a Shih Tzu and may not necessarily want to show their dogs but to anybody who is interested, is it an impossible dream or can anybody start to show?

Anyone can start to show and will enjoy it. To prepare, I recommend taking handling classes and grooming lessons with your Shih Tzu beforehand. The more you know about your breed, its care and maintenance and the handling of them, the better you will be in the show ring. Study your country's parent kennel club's official breed standard.

Gather information to include borrowing, purchasing publications such as this excellent book, periodicals about the breed, attending dog shows, speaking to exhibitors and breeders and attending the annual parent breed club's specialty show and visiting their websites.

In the U.S. it is the American Shih Tzu Club (ASTC) which offers an annual National Specialty and regional specialty shows at different locations across the country every year, as well as a wealth of online educational article material. Be sure to visit the ASTC online at:

http://www.americanshihtzuclub.org/

Most important are the early contacts you meet in getting started. For those who are getting serious about owning show quality Shih Tzu and preparing them for the experience, of great benefit would be having one or more mentors to guide you. These are fanciers who have a great deal of experience in breeding and showing, time to offer to you where they would be as objective as possible about quality assessment and be willing to put you through the paces in terms of grooming requirements and conformation training for optimal results.

The Shih Tzu is considered a high maintenance breed because of the hair and coat you must grow and condition to show them.

What really determines success at a dog show?

Some people say that success is when you've simply had fun at the show with your dog and other fanciers. You must have more than a long flowing coat and a love for your Shih Tzu, however, to win. As described in this book correctly, the Shih Tzu is a "head" breed. It is the whole of the dog to include form and function, balance, as compared to the official breed standard on its merits, not faults or weaknesses that ideally determines each individual dog's quality at a dog show. And, of course the Shih Tzu shown should have a fun-loving, showy personality, beautifully conditioned coat as described in the breed standard to befit its noble ancestry and correctly reflect the essence of the breed.

Success could be a class win, point win, and/or all the way to a Best in Show win. Each exhibitor determines what their level of success would be, even in smaller increments, at a dog show. For me, I've found that once you know what a truly sound, good specimen of the breed is and can reproduce it, improve or tweak for improvement/s is the ultimate success.

Showing dogs can become a costly hobby very often depending on how long it takes to complete a goal. While I enjoy showing my Shih Tzu breeder owner- handled, or owner-handled, I've found I cannot be away from home and my dogs to attend dog shows every weekend for practical reasons. I therefore need to hire a professional handler to help me reach my goals, as show frequency is important in terms of accumulating the necessary number of points and major wins for a championship title accomplishment. If I have done my homework with breeding, conditioning and training one of my Shih Tzu, certainly enough to show, I am going to aim for a championship title for those I've prepared for the experience.

Do you have any advice for people interested in showing?

Again, education is key. Learn about how dog shows are run, what you will need to do. The American Kennel Club offers rules and regulations to follow – you can order the booklet online at http://www.akc.org/. Many exhibitors are open to explain them to you as well as AKC representatives attending all of the AKC licensed dog shows.

Get the best dog or bitch you can find for a start, then commit to title completion. It's generally easier to show a male, as opposed to a female, because females can be hard on their coat and change behavior during their heat cycles.

Find your mentors, put time and money aside to participate in the sport and enjoy working with your dogs!

Don't forget that judges' assignments are to assess the breeding stock quality of the exhibits before them via the official breed standard description, observations on movement and their hands-on experience. There are good

Shih Tzu and judges and the opposite. Many owners have found that performance events, such as obedience, agility, rally, therapy dog, provide great satisfaction in lieu of conformation events. Shih Tzu are such a versatile, fun breed.

Coming away from the dog show aspect, why do you think people should choose the Shih Tzu breed over another breed of dog?

One of the initial attractions beyond the obvious from the darling, wide-eyed chrysanthemum puppy faces, to glamorous images we see in show photos is their expression and personality/temperament. That is what first interested me in this breed over others. Coupled with the size of this sturdy toy dog, they are a size which lends itself to easier mobility/transport with owners. A large dog personality in a smaller dog package best describes their personalities when correctly bred. What more could anyone ask for? I'm more than biased when I say that I think this breed offers owners a little heaven on earth as the best house and travel companions.

What advice would you give to people who are looking to buy a Shih Tzu dog?

Answer the questions honestly about ownership practicality. If you absolutely decide that yes, you are prepared to bring in a new family member into your home, I would endeavor to purchase the best quality you can find from a highly responsible breeder and please don't merely make your purchase from a photo you've seen on the internet!

Take your time to search and screen many breeders to find the best match for you and your family. You should be able to visit the breeder's premises and view their dogs. Make sure you have at least a verbal agreement, better yet to have a written agreement for improved clarity with the breeder so each (owner and breeder) knows what is expected of them. If you are interested in giving a rescue or foster Shih Tzu a new life, then please by all means. They too need loving, caring owners and good homes.

There are many different variations of Shih Tzu, what types do you think people should be looking at, or does it really not matter?

The word "types" can mean different things and characteristics to different people. Please study the breed standard and illustrated guide for Shih Tzu to get a better understanding of what the breed is supposed to encompass as correct examples. There is a reason for some subjective interpretation within the breed standard. Variation in the breed needs to exist to facilitate better opportunities within which to draw upon limited gene pools in order to work for the ideal representatives. Find physical specimens to study and notice the differences between them.

The ASTC offers an educational program where you can participate in a "hands-on" seminar where good examples and bad examples of the breed will be present for comparative analysis. It is presented by experienced breed experts with live dogs. I was the chairman of the breeder education committee who originally organized this free seminar in order to help anyone interested in learning more about the breed. The ASTC also offers hard copy Historical Record Books where you can see photos of past champions and their corresponding pedigrees.

The price of Shih Tzu seems to vary quite dramatically, do you think there is a minimum amount realistically that people should be spending?

Purchase price can certainly reflect the quality of the dogs, amount of time, effort and expense breeders have put into making and taking care of their adults and puppies. But price alone may not tell you what you will want to know about the breeder's care and quality they offer.
On the other hand, some breeders feel that a wonderful home for their dogs is worth perhaps a smaller price. As with any new addition to a family, the first task is finding the right fit/match to best suit your lifestyle and household and preparing a budget to accommodate him/her.

I don't feel anyone should be purchasing a Shih Tzu on a bargain basement basis simply because they want a dog without taking responsible ownership seriously and that means being a good provider for that dog's needs. You may be spending a smaller/lesser amount at the onset but the dog may also have serious issues which could be very expensive to solve during its lifetime with you.

What would you say are common mistakes that you have seen Shih Tzu owners make?

Underestimating this breed's intelligence is one of the most common mistakes made. Patience and a connection with your Shih Tzu when training is so important. Whether it's housebreaking or performance and event training, establishing a partnership which includes fun with productive activities, respect and a reward system are important. Common mistakes would be to assume that the dog will know what you mean when you haven't described a problem in such a way they can understand and punish them for it.

Personal experience directs me to learning and knowing more about canine behavior in general, how mothers relate to their young to train them, prepare them for life. Respecting your Shih Tzu as a valued dog goes a very long way to develop mutual respect which assists enormously in behavior modification when needed.

There seems to be some debate over nutrition and feeding, what are your routines such as how often and what types of food do you feed your Shih Tzu?

Feeding a smaller breakfast meal, a few treats midday and an evening supper to them has proven successful in my program. I feed a particular dry kibble where I've been told by one of my veterinarians that the company is one of the few to test their product continually before production and distribution. I've been satisfied with it and so have my dogs (it is Purina ProPlan adult and puppy for small dogs).

It's one of the only companies who have not experienced a food recall so far with their hard kibble. I think I spoil them however when I add deli shaved turkey from time to time, fresh veggies, and of course biscuits, treats. I also offer half of a pet tab as a supplement to those I am breeding and my new lactating mothers.

I know of many who recommend raw diets for their dogs but I still am fearful of the special refrigeration needs of this food to avoid e coli and salmonella. I would prefer cooked meat to avoid this risk.

Obviously grooming is another major aspect of owning a Shih Tzu, can you offer any tips, advice and perhaps some accessories that you wouldn't be without?

If you elect to groom our own pet at home, you will need to follow a schedule of clipping and trimming the hair and nails on a regular basis. I recommend at least a 6-8 week program, more often depending on the condition of your dog. Some items needed are an electric dryer (hand or stand), electric clipper, slicker brush, good trimming scissors, nail scissors, ear cleaning solution, sterile eye lubricant, shampoo and conditioner, styptic powder, cotton swabs, finger tooth brush and/or canine tooth brush, spray bottle for detangling solution, a pet pin brush and soft bristle brush.

Many owners of pet Shih Tzu choose to use a reliable and good groomer to schedule haircuts, baths, nail clipping and ear cleaning. Again, every 6-8 weeks is a good rule of thumb to make appointments, with baths and conditioning at home in between as needed.

All but the clippers mentioned above are used for a show coat with the addition of small face elastic bands, greyhound comb, a comb with a parting end for topknots, pin brushes with no head ends which tend to catch and pull the hair. I wouldn't be without my stand dryer, grooming table and grooming arm for my show Shih Tzu.

I would begin a daily check and face combing, re-banding as needed with elastics. Brush every other day when they come into more length of coat beginning at about 6-7 months. They will go through a puppy blow around 9 months. It's a time when they can mat and tangle fairly easily so daily brushing is needed.

I would not bathe full length show coats any more than every week to avoid stripping out all of the natural oils in the hair. When bathing, thoroughly rinse out the shampoo and almost rinse out the diluted conditioner you select to leave a slightly slick feel to the coat before you blow dry them. Use a clarifying shampoo every other or third bathing so as to eliminate too much product build up.

Much information and video material can be found online to help you with a step-by-step "how to" learning process when grooming the Shih Tzu for pet and for show.

You will need a lovely bow to finish the show topknot for the show. Face and coat staining can come from a variety of sources, namely air quality, hard water, food allergies and food additives can be the sources. The source for ear infection can also originate from food allergies and poor dental condition as well.

Are there any final thoughts that you feel the readers of this book would benefit from?

The Shih Tzu is one of the, if not THE, best breed we as people can own. It is through the hard work and dedication of responsible owners and breeders the breed continues with excellence.

Patronize only those with whom you feel comfortable and confident.

Love, love, love your Shih Tzu and they will send it and so much more right back to you!!

I wish to extend my thanks to my husband Paul, and daughter Emily, for their support and tolerance of me with my passion for my Shih Tzu hobby. Thank you also to my many great fancier friends who share in the craziness!!

Chapter 13 - Shih Tzu Breeders in the U.S.

Beautiful Valley Shih Tzu
Glen and Bonnie Cole
Leetonia, Ohio
http://www.beautifulvalleyshih-tzu.com

Intuition Shih Tzu
Kristie Miller
http://www.intuitionshihtzu.com/

Fantasy Shih Tzu
Susan Kilgore
Green Lake, WI 54941
http://www.fantasyshihtzu.com

JiDu De ShenTi Shih Tzu
Pam Crump
Corpus Christi, Texas
http://www.pamcrump.com

Lun Lynn Shih Tzu
Sherrie McGee
Unionville, Tennessee
http://www.lunlynnshihtzu.com

New York Shih Tzu Mom
Mary Anne Panko
Poughkeepsie, NY
http://www.newyorkshihtzu.com

Rocking K Shih Tzu
Regina Kitchens
Atlanta, Georgia
http://www.rockingkshihtzu.com

Sapphire Shih Tzu
Debi Buchholz
Kalispell, Montana
http://www.sapphireshihtzu.com

Scrumptious Shih Tzus
Lori Harmon
Springfield, Montana
http://www.scrumptiousshihtzus.com

Shih Tzu By The Shore
Edward Schott
Salisbury, MD
http://www.shihtzubytheshore.com

Sweetheart Shih Tzus
Lilly Masotto
Mountain Home, Arkansas
http://www.sweetheartshihtzus.com

Tallis Toy Dogs
Vida Ellis Hughes
Forsyth, Georgia
http://www.tallistoydogs.com

Chapter 14 - Shih Tzu Breeders in the UK

Fluffyangel
Mrs R & Mr J Rayner
Yorkshire
http://www.fluffyangelshihtzus.co.uk

Honeyshuchon Shih Tzus
Janine Scott
http://www.honeyshuchonshihtzus.co.uk

Jardhu Shih Tzu
Jim & Vikki Grugan,
http://www.jardhu.org.uk

Kamchat Shih Tzu's
Karen Morley
http://www.kamchatshihtzus.co.uk

Perfect Pups
Simone Brown
http://www.perfectpups.info

Rossvale
Sheila & Steve Brown
http://www.rossvale.co.uk

Shirkeira
Suzanne Kerée-Bartolo
http://www.shirkeira.com

Index

Lightning Source UK Ltd.
Milton Keynes UK
UKHW020803271220
375968UK00008B/179